Goldendo

Essential guide for Goldendoodle owners.

Goldendoodle book for training, care, costs, grooming and health.

By

Grace Weston

Table of Contents

Dedication

This is a dedication to all people who genuinely love and understand dogs, as well as a dedication to all dogs. Pure-bred, cross-bred, large and small!

Dogs are sentient beings that love unconditionally and rely totally on their owners for their wellbeing and survival. Unless you are willing to commit to a dog, to love it, take proper care of it and make it part of your family, don't get a dog!

I am a Forever Dog

Before you take me home, please understand
I am a forever dog
Not until you get bored with me dog
Not until you meet a boy/girl-friend dog
Not until when I get old or cost money dog
Not until when you have to move dog
Not until when you get a new puppy dog
Not until when you get pregnant dog
I am a forever dog
If you can't promise me forever
I am not your dog!

Author unknown

Introduction

Any true dog-lover understands the psychological and emotional bond that exists between dogs and human beings. This bond is believed to date back to over 100,000 years. The term 'man's best friend' is no casual expression for people who love and understand dogs; it is absolute!

Written by a life-long dog-lover, this book will not only discuss Goldendoodles, but reading between the lines you will find the love, commitment, and experience necessary to properly care for any dog, pure or mixed breed.

This book is not written for readers looking for scientific or expert facts. It is for dog-lovers who want to find out more about keeping a gorgeous Goldendoodle as a household pet and member of their family. For this reason, professional terms like 'bitch', 'dam' and 'sire' are replaced with the terms 'female', 'mother', 'male', 'father' and 'parents'. Terms are more befitting a Goldendoodle that will become part of your household and family.

There is no chapter on breeding with Goldendoodles because backyard breeding is greatly discouraged. To breed Goldendoodles ethically, you must be an expert on dog breeds, particularly Golden Retrievers and Poodles and dog genetics. You must be willing to invest a lot of money into creating a healthy and safe breeding environment before breeding begins. Puppies must be vaccinated and have regular veterinary health checks. They must be kept with their mother for a minimum of 8 weeks and up to 12 weeks before being sold. Breeding dogs is not a get-rich-quick scheme!

Rescue shelters and rescue groups are overcrowded with dogs bred by backyard breeders and puppy mills.

Have your Goldendoodle puppy spayed or neutered as soon as it is of age, which is between 4 to 6 months. Discuss the options with your vet before your puppy becomes of breeding age.

All dogs are pack animals that thrive in social environments, just like human beings. Although it may not be that obvious, people live in family groups (packs) and thrive in social environments (interaction with family and friends).

Goldendoodles, like all animals, are sentient beings that can feel pain (physical and emotional), fear, joy, sadness, depression, etc. - just like human beings. A Goldendoodle is not an object, an inanimate possession or a fashion statement. It cannot be cast aside when you are tired of it or have found something else to occupy your time.

Choosing to bring a Goldendoodle into your home and life is a daily commitment that can last for around 15 years. Only if you are totally prepared to make that commitment must you consider owning any dog! Once you have taken ownership of a dog, it will rely totally on you for its survival and wellbeing.

As a hybrid breed, Goldendoodles can be a fashion statement! If you want a Goldendoodle to show off with, you are on the wrong track. Fashions come and go; your responsibility to a dog lasts until it breathes its last breath.

Never buy a 'cute puppy' (Goldendoodle puppies are very cute) on impulse or as a gift for someone. A cute puppy quickly grows into a boisterous young dog. Many boisterous young Goldendoodles end up in shelters because their owners did not know how to handle them. Not all dogs that end up in shelters are adopted, and many pay the ultimate price of being euthanised because of some ignorant human being's irresponsible actions!

Also never buy a Goldendoodle to guard and protect your home and property, keeping them chained outside and left to sleep in an outside kennel. Any animal chained for any purpose is cruelty. Goldendoodles are particularly social animals! By keeping it chained, you are depriving it of all social interaction, adequate exercise and healthy dog behaviour like chasing around, digging and basking in the sun. Chained dogs often become aggressive or reclusive because of the mental agony of isolation, the lack of socialisation and the lack of human interaction. Anyone who keeps a dog on a chain day in and day out does not deserve to own a dog!

If you want a home protection system, invest in a camera security surveillance and alarm system. Those are inanimate objects that won't long for a gentle hand and a loving voice that will keep them company.

That said, let's look specifically at the gorgeous hybrid breed of dog, Goldendoodles. Goldendoodles are a very recent breed of dog resulting from cross-breeding a Golden Retriever with a Standard Poodle. The 'doodle' is derived from 'poodle' to avoid any confusion that the dog may be a 'golden poodle'.

Although there are records of Golden Retriever / Standard Poodle crossbreeds dating back to the late 1960's, Goldendoodles started gaining popularity as household pets in the 1990's when the breed name was named 'Goldendoodle'.

Initially, dog breeders began crossing Golden Retrievers with Standard Poodles with the specific intention of developing a breed of guide and service dogs for people with disabilities who also suffered from allergies to dogs.

Human allergy to dogs is usually to dander, which is skin protein that sheds from a dogs' skin together with dog hair. Allergies are sparked by the dander and not the actual hair shed. Poodles do not shed their coats very prolifically, so that reduces dander making them an almost hypoallergenic (relatively unlikely to cause an allergic reaction) breed.

Initially, Goldendoodles were only available from specific breeders, but since gaining popularity as household pets more than two decades ago, they are more readily available and can be found in pet stores and being sold through classified adverts online.

Goldendoodles are not a recognised breed, so there are no prescribed breed standards. They are considered to be hybrid or designer dogs that are bred specifically for various desirable characteristics. Because the breed is still very recent and there are no breed standards the coat type, colour, size, and temperament are not as predictable as with recognised purebred breeds that have a lineage going back for centuries in some cases.

Owning a Goldendoodle can be an adventure in some cases, and in other cases, you could have a wonderful family dog that fits into your household almost effortlessly.

Because of this, first-time or novice dog owners must do a lot of research into the background of a Goldendoodle puppy before they buy it. You can only get that in-depth information if you get the puppy from an ethical and registered breeder who knows both of the puppy's parents well. The breeder will be able to fill you in on the temperament and energy levels of both parents, and whether the puppy is genetically more like a Golden Retriever or a Poodle. You should be able to view both parents to see how they respond to you and if you believe that they have what you are looking for in a new puppy and ultimately a new member of your family. With the breeder's guidance and your viewing both parents, you should also be able to gauge the size that the puppy will eventually grow to and what temperament it should have.

There is a common myth that if you can add both parents height and weight together and then divide that sum by two and that will give you the height and weight your puppy will be in adulthood. Ignore this myth; genetics do not work that way! Genetics is a fascinating science, not a play by numbers game.

If you use the add and divide myth to estimate the adult size of your Goldendoodle puppy you could end up with a large dog that you thought would be a small dog. If you have limited space, a large and active dog could pose a problem.

For seasoned dog owners, venturing into unchartered waters and getting to know your Goldendoodle puppy as it matures can be interesting and quite an adventure. Seasoned dog-owners can easily estimate the size that the Goldendoodle puppy will reach in adulthood by looking at its bone structure.

If after reading this book you choose to add a gorgeous Goldendoodle to your household, may it become a much loved, valued and integral part of your family!

Chapter 1: Goldendoodle History

Before you look at the actual Goldendoodle breed, you must first understand their lineage because they are still a very recent breed. It is quite likely that the Goldendoodle puppy you choose could have been bred directly from a Golden Retriever and Poodle crossing, or be a second or third generation. The characteristics of the original breeds will still feature very prominently in your Goldendoodle. Characteristics of size, coat and temperament can vary greatly in this recent breed. Even littermates can display a noted difference in characteristics depending on the genes that each puppy has inherited.

1. Golden Retrievers

The Golden Retriever is a large, thick-set strong breed of dog that originated in Scotland sometime in the late 1800's. They were initially bred as gun-dogs and trained to retrieve and return any hunted birds or small mammals to the shooter undamaged.

They are very easy to train and will learn basic commands from a young age, progressing quickly to advanced commands. They excel in obedience training.

a) Weight and Height

Although breed standards vary as Golden Retrievers have been exported and standardised in different countries, their average height and weight can be expected to be:

Males

- Weight –29 to 34 Kilograms or 65 to 75 Pounds
- Shoulder Height – 56 to 61 Centimetres or 22 to 24 Inches

Females

- Weight – 25 to 29 Kilograms or 55 to 65 Pounds
- Shoulder Height – 51 to 56 Centimetres or 20 to 22 Inches

b) Temperament

Golden Retrievers are even-tempered and well-behaved dogs. They are a social breed of dog and need constant companionship (canine, human or other animals) to bond with and play.

They thrive in human company and on being included in a family environment. If excluded from the family environment or left alone for long periods of time they can develop destructive behaviour patterns like chewing on furniture, uprooting your garden, overturning dustbins and compost bins, etc.

Golden Retrievers do well with children, but their big size may unintentionally hurt small children and toddlers resulting in a negative reaction from the child. Small children must never be without adult supervision around any dog breed.

Older children make excellent playmates for golden retrieves because they enjoy running, swimming, retrieving sticks, balls, Frisbees, etc. They are also excellent jogging companions.

Golden Retrievers are great 'chewers' inside the house and outside. It is essential that you always provide them with lots of toys, dog chews, hooves, etc. to prevent them from chewing and destroying your furniture, carpets, wheelie-bin (yes, they are big dogs), shoes, towels and anything else they stumble upon.

Their gentle temperament makes them excellent family pets, and they are a popular choice for a pet worldwide. They are good watch dogs, so they will immediately alert you if there is anything untoward happening within the home, but they have no guarding instinct.

c) Exercise

Because they are a large breed and bred for hunting, Golden Retrievers need a lot of exercise. They are well suited to urban living, but unless you have a large property that allows them ample running space, they do need to be taken for long walks daily or taken for an extended run in a park.

Golden Retrievers have an instinctive love for water and will dive into any pool of water at the first opportunity they get. If you don't have a pool for them at home, a regular trip to a park with a lake or dam will make a wonderful treat.

To maintain their health and fitness, adult Golden Retrievers need a minimum of two hours vigorous exercise every day. Without enough regular exercise, Golden Retrievers gain weight and can become obese which could lead to health problems.

d) Training

Golden retrievers train very easily, and their gentle temperament has led to them being used extensively as guide dogs for people who are visually impaired, hearing dogs for people who are deaf and as disability assistance dogs for people with other disabilities. They also make very good detection, and search and rescue dogs and are widely used for these purposes by military, police and rescue services worldwide.

e) Coat and Grooming

As their name indicates, the coat of a Golden Retriever varies from light golden to dark golden. They have a thick, long coat that comprises two layers. The inner layer is dense and provides insulation for their body to keep them warm in cold weather and cool in hot weather. The outer layer has a slight kink and lies flat against their body to repel water. The outer coat sheds slightly throughout the year. Both layers of coat shed excessively at the change of seasons.

Golden Retrievers require regular grooming and occasional baths. Because their coats shed slightly throughout the year, they should be brushed to remove dead hair from their coat at least twice a week. At the change of season when they shed excessively, daily brushing is advised to remove the dead hair. Daily brushing means less hair dropped around your house or inside your vehicle.

Their coat can grow quite long, particularly on the legs, tail, and underbelly. Clipping some of the length off makes it easier them and for you, as their coat is less likely to become entangled in the undergrowth and pick up dead bits of plant material as well as parasites.

f) Health and Lifespan

All healthy dogs should be taken to a vet at least once a year for vaccinations and a general health check. As they age, they should visit the vet more frequently for a complete health check.

Golden Retrievers are known to have genetic disorders and to be susceptible to certain health conditions. Hip and Elbow Dysplasia are very common in the breed. The conditions are treatable.

Ear infections are also common. Wipe their ears out regularly and if there is any bad odour or discharge, an immediate visit to the vet is required.

They are also inclined to allergies (generally to fleas), which can cause Acute Moist Dermatitis (hot-spots). Checking for fleas should be done while brushing. Quality flea control products are readily available from specialist pet product retailers and vets. Discuss treating hotspots with your vet.

There are three genetic eye diseases in Golden Retrievers that can lead to blindness. These are Cataracts, Progressive Retinal Atrophy, and Uveitis. Of the three, Uveitis is the most common. Briefly described:

- Uveitis is an intraocular inflammation. Genetic Uveitis presents with inflammation of the conjunctiva, colour change of the iris, squinting, abnormal pupil shape and cloudiness of the eye. Treatment depends on the stage of the disease. If identified in the early stages, dogs can be prescribed life-long treatment that will halt the progress of the disease, and save their vision.

- Cataracts are an opacity within the lens of the eye. A healthy lens is clear and used for focusing. Any opacity will affect vision. Cataracts can develop in a dog at any age although they are more common in older dogs. Either one or both eyes can be affected. Cataracts develop in three stages, namely immature, mature and hyper-mature. The effect the cataract has on the dog's vision will range from slightly blurred to very blurred and ultimately blindness. Cataracts can be removed surgically.

- Progressive Retinal Atrophy is an inherited genetic disease that can affect a dog at any age. It is a disease of the retina that causes rod-cells in the retina to die. It occurs in both eyes simultaneously and isincurable. Ultimately it leads to total blindness. There are life-long prescription medications that can slow down the progress of blindness.

Because of their tendency to gain weight if overfed and not exercised enough, Golden Retrievers are inclined to obesity-related diseases.

Although the breed is inclined to weight gain, weight control lies completely within the domain of the owners' responsibility. If any dog becomes obese, the owner is the cause!

Common causes of death in the breed are cancer and heart disease.

The average lifespan of a Golden Retriever is 11 to 12 years.

2. Poodles

Poodles are intelligent, active, squarely built and elegant with a curly coat. They are bred in four sizes, namely: Standard, Medium, Miniature, and Toy.

Records depict Poodles in paintings dating back to the 1600's. However, the origin of the breed is under dispute. Some trace the origins back to Germany and others to France. Either way, the Poodle has a long history on the European continent as a hunting dog used for retrieving game birds and small mammals from water and in the field and returning it to the hunter undamaged.

Today Standard, Medium and even Miniature and Toy Poodles are used as hunting dogs. Toy sized Poodles are used for hunting and sniffing out truffles. Irrelevant of the size, they share the same traits innate to the breed.

Miniature and Toy sizes were initially bred to be human companion dogs. However, their intelligence and ease of training soon had bird hunters recognising the value of the small size to find prey trapped in small places where the larger dogs are unable to reach. Truffle hunters also recognised the value of the Miniature and Toy sizes to sniff out sites where truffles grow.

Standard Poodles have worked as service dogs in the military since the 1700's, and over the past century, they have worked as service dogs in the navy and coast guard.

a) Temperament

Poodles are highly intelligent, energetic and sociable, requiring exercise and mental stimulation. Their instinctive hunting trait is present in all sizes, so it must be expected that they are inclined to chase birds, rodents, squirrels, etc. around your property. In many Poodles, the instinctive drive to hunt will result in a relentless pursuit of their prey. They can be easily trained to obey commands, so if your Poodle displays this trait, you can introduce commands that will tell it to back-off. It will also be best to bring your Poodle indoors for a while to allow their chosen prey to beat a hasty retreat!

They are not innately aggressive dogs and are more inclined to be reserved when encountering strangers than running in to attack. Once they are comfortable with people in their surroundings, they are relaxed and amiable. Overall Poodles have a kind demeanour.

Standard and Medium sized Poodles are better suited to homes with smaller children because they love playing games and running around. They will readily accompany a family on a hiking trip and any activity involving water sport.

Small and Toy sized poodles are best suited to homes with older children who understand how to treat a small dog. They enjoy playing games and having a good run, but their small size limits their ability to handle rough play. They also don't take kindly to small (well-intentioned) children hugging them and carrying them around. Supervise small children around dogs - always! If a small child (who appears very big to a Small or Toy sized dog) picks the Poodle up in a manner that makes the little dog feel threatened it might snap or nip.

All Poodles want to be part of the family and can be prone to anxious behaviour if excluded. They don't like being left alone and can be inclined to separation anxiety.

Their kind temperament makes them excellent family pets, and they are a popular choice for pet worldwide. They are good watch dogs, so they will immediately alert you if there is anything untoward happening within the home, but they have no guarding instinct.

b) Exercise

All Poodles are well suited to urban living. An adult Poodle of any size needs a minimum of an hour of vigorous exercise every day. Poodles are active dogs, so regular exercise is essential to their physical and mental wellbeing.

Standard and Medium poodles obviously need more exercise, and from Standard to Toy, they all love water so a regular swim will be most welcome. Standard and Medium sized poodles make excellent jogging partners.

If you have a large property with ample running space, all four sizes will get enough exercise without daily walks. If your property does not have very much running space, you will have to take your Standard or Medium sized Poodle for daily walks. If you live in an apartment that has no outdoor running space, you will have to walk your Small or Toy sized Poodle daily as well.

Standard and Medium sized Poodles should never be kept in an apartment environment. Poodles are active dogs, and an apartment is too cramped for a Standard or Medium sized Poodle's health and wellbeing.

c) Training

Because they are highly intelligent, Poodles are easily trained and excel at obedience training. The Standard and Medium sizes do very well in all dog sports and competitions and can handle vigorous and extensive activities that involve mental and physical stimulation. The Small and Toy sizes also enjoy physical activities that involve mental stimulation, but their small size must be taken into consideration when choosing activities.

Poodles have a keen working intelligence. They are excellent swimmers and are athletic in build and stamina. Poodles have a drive and independence that sets them apart from the other 'retriever' breeds, so they can wander off and do their own thing! They need to be trained very well to follow commands from a young age. Poodles are however very eager to please, so early training will eliminate their independent drive.

Because of their intelligence and kind demeanour, training must be precise and firm, but exercised with a kind hand. Reward commands that are understood. Your Poodle will respond very well because of their eagerness to please. Correct mistakes or misunderstandings with precise repetitive commands in a firm voice with distinct hand gestures. There must be no shouting, aggression, punishment or overbearing gestures; this can cause the poodle to become fearful and freeze-up. No further training will be possible for the rest of the day. Exposing a Poodle repeatedly to harsh and punitive training methods could make it become withdrawn and shy away from human company.

d) Coat and Grooming

Unlike other water breeds that have a double layered coat, Poodles have a single layered coat. There is no undercoat. Their coat is dense and curly, and shedding is minimal. The hair that sheds does not fall from the Poodle but instead becomes entangled in the coat. Poodles are considered to be a hypoallergenic breed, but not completely allergen free.

Because the dead hair becomes entangled in the coat, regular brushing is essential otherwise the coat can become matted. Clipping and shaving are recommended to prevent matting and bits of undergrowth and parasites becoming entangled in the coat. A visit to a grooming parlour every six to eight weeks is adequate to keep your Poodles' coat in good condition.

Poodles' coat ranges from coarse and woolly to soft and curly. Coat colours range from pure white to pitch black as well as golden to chocolate. Patched coats are also common.

There are many different styles of clipping a Poodle's coat. Some clipping styles originated for practical purposes and others for show. As a household pet, how you choose to clip your poodle's coat is a matter of personal choice.

e) Health

All healthy dogs should be taken to a vet at least once a year for vaccinations and a general health check. As they age, they should visit the vet more frequently for a complete health check.

All size of Poodles are inclined to ear infections so wipe their ears out regularly. If there is any bad odour or discharge an immediate visit to the vet is required.

Hip and Elbow Dysplasia is very common in the breed. The conditions are treatable.

There are genetic eye diseases in all sizes of Poodles that can lead to blindness. These are Cataracts, Progressive Retinal Atrophy, Optic Nerve Hypoplasia and Glaucoma. Briefly described:

- Cataracts in Poodles form, grow and can be treated exactly as with Golden Retrievers.
- Progressive Retinal Atrophy is an inherited genetic disease that progresses andcan be treat exactly as with Golden Retrievers.
- Optic Nerve Hypoplasia is also a genetically inherited disease that disrupts and deteriorates ocular activity. The disease is more ruthless than other progressive eye because puppies that have inherited the condition are born partially or totally blind. The only advantage to this is that the puppy will learn from birth to better develop its other senses to cope with its blindness.
- Glaucoma is another genetically inherited disease that causes a build-up of fluid in the back of the dog's eye. The fluid applies pressure to the sensitive ocular nerves that connect the eyes to the brain. Eventually, this pressure can cause partial or total blindness. If diagnosed early there are life-long prescription medications that can slow down the progress of blindness.

Poodles are also inclined to Addison's disease, which can be fatal if left untreated. It is more prevalent in females and is caused by a reduction corticosteroid secretion from the adrenal gland. If diagnosed early it can be treated with life-long medication to control physiological imbalances.

Also, they are inclined to Gastric Dilatation-Volvulus or a twisted stomach. Unless there is immediate veterinary intervention, this condition is fatal.

vonWillebrand's disease is also found in Poodles' genetics. It is a blood disorder characterised by unusual, prolonged bleeding. It can cause nosebleeds, bleeding from the gums and occasionally blood in the faeces. Prolonged bleeding after surgery and during heat cycles after whelping are also common. It can be treated with life-long medication. Left untreated it can be fatal.

Epilepsy can be found in Poodle's genetics and can be treated with life-long medication if not severe. Repeated severe epileptic seizures can cause brain damage, and the quality of the dog's life must be consideration these instances.

Tracheal collapse, renal disease, and cancer are also causes of death in poodles.

3. Poodles Weight and Height

Kennel Club standards vary from country to country, so an average has been taken to give an estimated guide. Height determines Poodle sizes, not weight.

a) Standard Poodle

- Weight - 20 to 32 Kilograms or 45 to 70 Pounds
- Shoulder Height - 45 to 60 Centimetres or 18 to 24 Inches
- Lifespan -11 to 12 years

b) Medium Poodles (Not recognised by all Kennel Clubs)

- Weight -10 to 12 Kilograms or 22 to 26 Pounds
- Shoulder Height - 35 to 45 Centimetres or 14 to 18 Inches
- Lifespan - 12 to 13 years

c) Miniature Poodles

- Weight - 6 to 7 Kilograms or 15 to 17 Pounds
- Shoulder Height - 28 to 38 Centimetres or 11 to 15 Inches
- Lifespan - 14 to 15 years

d) Toy Poodles

- Weight - 3 to 4 Kilograms or 6 to 9 Pounds
- Shoulder Height - 24 to 27 Centimetres or 9 to 11 Inches
- Lifespan - 14 to 15 years

Chapter 2: About Goldendoodles

As stated in the Introduction, Goldendoodles are a very recent hybrid breed of dog resulting from crossing a Golden Retriever with a Standard Poodle. The breeders' initial idea was to create a hypoallergenic service dog for people with allergies to dog dander.

As the breed started becoming popular as household pets, breeders began breeding smaller Goldendoodles by crossing Golden Retrievers with the smaller sized Poodles.

Unfortunately, it has not taken long for backyard breeders and puppy mills to jump on the bandwagon, introducing indiscriminate breeding practices that often result in puppies with unstable temperaments or congenital disabilities.

A well-bred Goldendoodle should have a gentle nature, be intelligent and easy to train, be energetic and active and should make an excellent human companion. These are inherent characteristics of both Golden Retrievers and Poodles.

Unless you have a large property with ample running space, it is best to buy your new puppy from a reputable breeder. Goldendoodles can grow into large dogs if they have inherited their genes from their Golden Retriever parentage or the Standard Poodle. Both of the pure-bred parents, grand or great-grandparents are large, active dogs. A puppy may look small when still only a few weeks old, but within a few months, you could find yourself with a dog that is too big for your home and property. That is a position you don't want to find yourself in or put any dog that has bonded with your family in either. The outcome could lead to heartbreak on all sides!

A reputable breeder who knows both parents will be able to give you the approximate size that the puppy will reach in adulthood based on the puppy's anatomy including, paw and skull size as well as the circumference of certain long bones. The estimate might not be exact, but at least you will know if you are buying a small, medium or large dog.

1. Large Goldendoodles

A large Goldendoodle is either a first, second, third or maybe fourth generation descendent of a crossing between a Golden Retriever and a Standard Poodle.

It is a large dog and can stand from 56 to 61 Centimetres or 22 to 24 Inches at shoulder height and weight from 20 to 34 Kilograms or 45 to 75 Pounds.

Because the bloodline is mixed and breed standards for Golden Retrievers and Standard Poodles vary from one country to another, the size and weight estimates are a mere guideline.

It could have the strong, thick-set build of the Golden Retriever or the square-set elegance of the Standard Poodle. If it has inherited the build of the Golden Retriever, it will have a broader skull than that of the Poodle. Both Golden Retrievers and Standard Poodles have long legs and are athletic in appearance.

2. Medium Goldendoodles

Much the same as the Large Goldendoodle, a Medium Goldendoodle is either a first, second, or maybe third generation descendent of a crossing between a Golden Retriever and a Medium Poodle. Medium Goldendoodles were bred in more recent years for the family pet market.

It is a medium-sized dog and can stand from 43 to 51 Centimetres 17 to 20 inches at shoulder height and weight from 18 to 23 Kilograms or 40 to 50 pounds.

Because the bloodline is mixed and breed standards for Golden Retrievers and Standard Poodles vary from one country to another, the size and weight estimates are a mere guideline.

Although smaller and lighter than the Large Goldendoodle, a Medium Goldendoodle could have the strong, thick-set build of the Golden Retriever or the square-set elegance of the Standard Poodle. If it has inherited the build of the Golden Retriever, it will also have a broader skull than that of the Poodle. Both Golden Retrievers and Medium Poodles have long legs and are athletic in build.

3. Small Goldendoodles

Small Goldendoodles have made an even more recent appearance on the pet scene and are most likely a first or second generation descendent of a crossing between a Golden Retriever and a Miniature Poodle. Small Goldendoodles have been bred as family pets, particularly for apartment living.

Many breeders use artificial insemination as a means of conception. Bearing in mind that genetics within the same litter can vary greatly in hybrid breeds if the female giving birth is of a frail build and is carrying a puppy or puppies who have inherited the more thick-set bone structure of the Golden Retriever, she could encounter birthing problems. Most puppy mill breeders will not be willing to pay for a caesarean birth.

A Small Goldendoodle is a small-sized dog and can stand from 33 to 50 centimetres or 13 to 20 inches at shoulder height and weight from 7 to 14 kilograms or 15 to 30 pounds.

Because the bloodline is mixed and breed standards for Golden Retrievers and Standard Poodles vary from one country to another, the size and weight estimates are a mere guideline.

Although smaller and lighter than the Medium Goldendoodle, it could have the strong, thick-set build of the Golden Retriever or the square-set elegance of the standard poodle. If it has inherited the build of the Golden Retriever, it will have a broader skull than that of the Poodle. It will have long legs and an athletic in appearance.

4. Coat Types and Colours

Most Goldendoodle puppies have quite a flat, even-lengthed coat for the first few weeks of their life. In later weeks, their coat will start to curl or become wavy, displaying first indications of their adult.

Once the puppies' adult coat starts to grow, it can range from tightly curled, curly through to wavy and it should grow to about 5 to 8 centimetres or 2 to 3 inches in length. The hair on their ears, legs, lower sides, tail, and under-belly tends to be longer while the hair on their head and muzzle tends to be shorter. The hair on their legs may be fine and feathery.

The Goldendoodles coat come in a wide range of colours from black to grey, white, cream, golden, apricot, copper and red. Some Goldendoodles coats are a solid colour with white feathering. The most common colour is golden - from light to dark.

The coat texture, colour, and shedding are still unpredictable even if the Goldendoodle has been bought from a breeder. The breed lineage is too recent to have isolated and excluded specific features like shedding, coat texture, etc.

If you are looking to add a Goldendoodle to your family specifically for its potentially hypoallergenic qualities, you must buy from a reputable breeder. Select a puppy with a single layer coat like a Poodle because that puppy has likely inherited the Poodle genes that result is less shedding and less dander, although that cannot be guaranteed. The breeder will be able to identify puppies that have a 'Poodle' type coat.

Chapter 3: Is a Goldendoodle Right for You?

Because Goldendoodles are still a very recent hybrid breed, first-time and novice dog owners must ensure that they are very comfortable with the breed characteristics before bringing a Goldendoodle puppy home.

Both Golden Retrievers and Poodles were bred as working dogs and are still widely used in various roles as working and service dogs. Both breeds have gentle, kind natures and are very easy to train because they want to please. Both breeds need to be part of a social group, and that social group will be your family. Exclusion from the family environment can lead to destructive or obsessive behaviours or depression.

That both breeds in the Goldendoodles lineage have a gentle, kind nature and need includsion in a family is a very important factor. Your Goldendoodle puppy is almost certainly going to inherit this trait. They need to be part of the family, and that means living inside the house with the family and partaking in family activities. They do not take well to being excluded or locked out of the house for extended periods of time.

Also, both Golden Retrievers and Poodles are intelligent dogs, so that means that they do not only require daily physical exercise but daily mental stimulation as well. Failure to provide a Goldendoodle with plenty of opportunity for physical exercise and mental stimulation will also lead to destructive or obsessive behaviours or depression.

First-time or novice dog owners who understand very little of the behaviour of dogs in general, may battle with training and misinterpret the Goldendoodles sociable and intelligent behaviour as 'naughty' or 'difficult'.

Many pure-bred, expensive dogs end up as unwanted in shelters because the people who bought them bought them for the wrong reasons and made no effort to understand the breed characteristics.

You need to sit down as a family and discuss openly and honestly if you are all 'dog-people'! You must ask if you are all happy with a dog that lives inside the house? A dog that wants to watch television with you? A dog that wants to share your space while you are busy with household chores? A dog that wants to be with you when you are relaxing or having a meal? (Being with you while you are having a meal does not mean sharing your meal; all dog breeds can be trained not to beg for food). Are you willing to have a dog sleep in the house (not necessarily in your bed, but somewhere inside the house in its own bed)?

Remember, having a dog or dogs living in your house means that your whole family will have to make certain concessions. This fact must be thought through very well because it can't become a consideration once you have brought a Goldendoodle puppy home. Some concessions are:

- The four-legged fury is a constant presence in the house; a very constant presence
- When it is a puppy, it will have to be house-trained which requires dedicated patience and effort, just like potty-training a human baby
- When it gets older, it will slip up occasionally, particularly in cold, wet weather, leaving you cleaning up a wee or poop
- Regular grooming is essential if your Goldendoodle lives in your house
- Internal and external parasite control (worms, fleas and ticks) is essential if your Goldendoodle lives in your house
- It will be curious and want to know what you are doing, often pushing its nose right into what you are busy with; it needs to be included, not pushed away and shouted at
- If the doorbell or phone rings it will be first at the point of call; it is curious and sociable
- It will follow family members around the house; it is curious
- It will constantly attempt to communicate with you and draw your attention; it is intelligent
- If allowed on the furniture, your favourite seat could be taken for the next 10 to 15 years; dogs have a way like that, and you end up moving, not them
- If you work in the garden, it will offer uninvited assistance
- When it rains, you will have to clean muddy paw prints from the floor, carpet and furniture
- It may snore while you are watching your favourite television program or movie (waking it does not help; it will just look at you and return to snoring)
- It has to be taken for long walks daily unless you own a very large property
- It has to have daily mental stimulation, so playing games like 'fetch' or hiding treats around the house or garden are a must
- If you get visitors it won't take well to being locked out; it will perform, whine and scratch at doors, etc.

- You will have to include it when visitors come around (a well-trained dog will pay visitors attention for the first few minutes and then go about its's usual business)

These are just some of the concessions that dog-people make every day for their furry family member/s, but not everyone is a dog-person. If anyone in your family is not able to make these concessions as well as a whole lot more, then a Goldendoodle is not for your family because the breed thrives on human companionship.

You cannot buy a Goldendoodle puppy and keep it in the house while it's small and cute and then exclude it from the family by leaving it outside once it becomes too 'difficult' or 'too big'. Not only is that irresponsible pet ownership, but you will kill its spirit. Remember, Goldendoodles are bred from gentle, kind natured breeds that need human company.

Think very carefully and make an honest decision. A sentient, beautiful dog's mental health and overall well-being depends on what you decide!

1. Not just an Adorable Face

Goldendoodles are not just an adorable face because behind that face is an intelligent, affectionate friend offering total dedication, love and companionship to you for the next 10 to 15 years. But that's not all - behind that face is a mischievous, fun-loving, intelligent dog that needs physical exercise, mental stimulation, love and companionship. In other words, Goldendoodles need to be played with, walked, spoken to and given love and cuddles to keep them happy.

In return, you will have hours of entertainment, unconditional love, dedication, companionship and genuine friendship. Goldendoodles are gentle, kind and patient, so they make excellent companion dogs.

Obviously, no one can dedicate all their time to a dog, so the idea is to make them part of the family where they live alongside everyone else. It will take some early training to get them to follow the family routines, but for the most part, they are easy to train and want to please so they should fit in quickly.

Because they need mental stimulation and like to play, make sure you offer them a variety of toys and dog chews to keep them busy. If you don't, they will find mental stimulation and play elsewhere, like chewing up toilet rolls, furniture, shoes, etc.

Unless you work from home or are at home all day, it is best to have more than one dog so that they can play together and keep each other company while you are away. Dogs that have a canine companion or two are not as demanding as one dog. Goldendoodles' gentle nature inclines them to accept other animals like cats as well. A Goldendoodle/cat bond could very easily work well too.

2. Temperament

Bred from two species that thrive in human company and service, Goldendoodles, for the most part, make excellent family pets. Their size does dictate the type of family environment that will suit them best.

Large and Medium Goldendoodles are best suited to an active family environment that offers a lot of outdoor sport and play where they can join in. Lots of love and attention, active play, and ample running space are essential. Because of the height of a Large Goldendoodle, the outside yard must be secured with high fencing or walls, because a large active dog could easily jump over a low enclosure.

Large and Medium Goldendoodles are not suited to apartment living.

Small Goldendoodles are also suited to an active family environment, but small children must only be allowed to play with a Small Goldendoodle under adult supervision. Because of their small size, boisterous over-zealous attention from a little person can seem quite intimidating to a small dog. The most likely outcome will be that your Goldendoodle will run and hide somewhere, but in some cases, it may nip or snap.

Small Goldendoodles are well suited to apartment living as long as they are walked daily and are not left alone for extended periods of time.

It is very uncharacteristic for Goldendoodles to be aggressive and they do not make good watchdogs. All dogs have an instinctive sense of guarding their pack and territory, so if anything untoward happens within your property - inside or outside, your Goldendoodle will most likely alert you by barking. They should however never be brought home to be a watchdog.

Goldendoodles may be either curious or shy of strangers, but it's most unlikely that they would attack a stranger. It may take them a while to warm up to visitors, but if the visitors ignore them, obviously opposing no threat, curiosity will get the better of your Goldendoodle. They might approach the visitors with caution, or they might become very friendly very quickly. After a gentle pat and kind 'hello' from your visitors your Goldendoodle will accept them and then, for the most part, go about its business as usual.

You will notice the regular use of the terms 'generally' and 'for the most part'. It is intentional because Goldendoodles are a hybrid breed and there are no set standards for characteristics and temperament. Behaviour can vary quite vastly from one individual to another.

It is highly recommended to buy from a registered and reputable breeder who will sell you a genuine Goldendoodle. Backyard breeders and puppy mills are not ethical, and they may sell puppies as Goldendoodles that are not from a pure-bred Golden Retriever/Poodle cross. In such cases, the puppy may have aggressive traits inherited genetically from a more aggressive breed of dog.

3. Energy Level and Exercise

Large Goldendoodles are more active than the smaller Goldendoodles simply because they are bigger! Large Goldendoodles need at least an hour of vigorous activity and exercise every day. If you have a large property, they could get this exercise by just running around and playing, particularly if they have another canine companion or active children. If your property is not very big, you will have to take your large and medium Goldendoodle for daily walks.

Both large and medium Goldendoodles make excellent jogging companions, and they will also do well on family hikes or picnics.

Small Goldendoodles also need daily exercise, but if they live indoors and you have an outside yard to run in, they should get enough exercise by running around and from play, particularly if they too have another canine companion. If you live in an apartment, you will have to take them for daily walks.

Older Goldendoodles do become less active. All sizes are genetically inclined to Hip and Elbow Dysplasia, and this can affect a Goldendoodle of any age. It is vital that you keep a lookout for any signs of joint pain, reluctance to jump or climb stairs, limping or a 'hopping' gait and reduced activity. Hip and elbow dysplasia are treatable, and the sooner the condition is diagnosed, the easier the treatment. If you suspect your Goldendoodle has hip or elbow dysplasia, take it to your vet as soon as possible.

4. Grooming

It is important that you make grooming a regular activity from the time that you bring your Goldendoodle home as a puppy. The best way to get your Goldendoodle hooked on regular grooming from a puppy is to turn a grooming session into an interactive play session. Speak to your puppy, tell it what you are doing, encourage it to stand still, and when it does give it praise. When all is done and dusted, compliment it on its good looks.

If you think a Goldendoodle cannot accept a compliment you are going to be surprised. Just look at the expression on that face when you say "Look how beautiful you look now!"

If you introduce your puppy to weekly grooming sessions from the get-go, it can become an ideal opportunity to also give your Goldendoodle a good look-over while grooming to check for any health issues or parasites like fleas and ticks. Looking for any inflammation, tenderness and open skin on the body, paws (including pads), nose, ears, and eyes can help you pick up any potential health issues early on.

Your Goldendoodle could have the coat of a Golden Retriever which is double layered and wavy or a Poodle which is single layered and ranges from coarse and woolly to soft and curly.

Although Goldendoodles are considered light shedders, not all have inherited the almost hypoallergenic non-shedding coat of the poodle.

Either way, their coat requires regular weekly brushing. If your Goldendoodle does shed, it's best to brush it at least twice a week. If they do not shed much like the Poodle, weekly brushing is essential to avoid matting.

If you brush your Goldendoodle's coat regularly, natural oils in the skin will keep the coat clean and healthy. A bath every 6 to 8 weeks is adequate.

It is advised to clip your Goldendoodles coat to prevent matting, to prevent bits of undergrowth becoming entangled in the coat and prevent parasites from clinging to the coat. Clipping can be just cutting back the long feathering on the legs, or you can have your Goldendoodle clipped at a dog parlour. Fancy clipping styles are not necessary, and Goldendoodles look adorable in their natural state with areas of long hair clipped for practical purposes only.

In addition to brushing your Goldendoodles coat, you should also brush its teeth two or three times a week to prevent gum disease and tartar build-up. Brushing its teeth is definitely something that must be introduced when your Goldendoodle is still a puppy. Very few dogs will take well to having their teeth brushed if they are only introduced to a toothbrush as an adult. Dogs don't like having their mouth forced open.

Because Goldendoodles are inclined to ear infections, do a thorough check of the inside of your Goldendoodles ears every time you brush it. Wipe the inside of the ears clean with a damp cloth and dry well. Any inflammation, discharge or odour calls for an immediate trip to the vet. Ear ache is a very painful condition.

If your Goldendoodles toenails do not get worn down naturally, you will have to clip them. It can be a very tricky job for the uninitiated because dogs, like humans, have a live nail-bed that contains blood vessels. If the nails are cut too short, it will cause pain and bleeding. If you are unsure where the nail-bed begins, it's best to take your Goldendoodle to a dog parlour or vet to have its nails clipped.

A dog's toenails will grow too long if they do not have a rough surface that they can walk and run on daily. It is common for inactive dogs and dogs that live in apartments without being taken for regular walks along pavements and in parks.

Chapter 4. Cost of Keeping a Goldendoodle

1. A Dog License

Having a license to own a dog is not mandatory in all countries, and in some countries, it is mandatory in some states or provinces and not in others. If in doubt, check with your local council.

Each country, province or state where dog licenses are mandatory attach a different set of rules and costs to the license. Listed below are a few countries and the rules that apply to dog licenses.

a) Australia

Dog licenses are mandated by state and territory legislation, but issued by local government. The cost of a dog license and the format of the license tags vary across the country. There are, however, certain criteria that apply across the board to owning a dog in Australia, and full compliance with these regulations are mandatory to obtain a dog license. These include:

- All dogs aged 12 weeks and older must be registered at the local council
- Dogs must be micro-chipped
- If you have acquired a puppy, it must be micro-chipped before registration at the local council
- The council registration tag must be attached to a collar that must be worn permanently around your dog's neck
- You have to register every dog that you own separately
- Registrations must be renewed annually

Dog owners who fail to register their dogs or comply with the licence requirements can face a fine. The fine differs between local governments.

Spaying and neutering dogs is a pre-requisite to obtaining a dog license in some local government areas.

b) Canada

Dog licenses are mandatory in most cities in Canada, but the cost and pre-requisites differ from city to city. The municipality in each city sets the prerequisite regulations with some municipalities offering an optional discount on dog license fees for veterinary proof that a dog has been spayed or neutered, and others making spaying and neutering a prerequisite. The age at which a dog must be licenced also varies from city to city.

Micro-chipping a dog is mandatory in most cities in Canada and dog licenses must be renewed annually. Each dog that you own needs to be licensed separately.

Failure to licence a dog or renew a licence in cities where licensing in mandatory can result in a fine.

c) Great Britain

Dog licenses were abolished in Great Britain in 1987. It is a requirement in Great Britain that all dogs be micro-chipped.

d) Ireland

Dog licenses are mandatory in Ireland and Northern Ireland. There are three types of dog licenses:

- Individual dog license that covers a dog for 12 months
- General dog license for kennel owners for 12 months
- Lifetime of a dog license that covers a dog for its lifetime

Discounts on license fees are offered to pensioners and people who provide veterinary proof that a dog has been spayed or neutered.

Failure to licence a dog or renew a 12-month licence can result in a fine.

e) New Zealand

It is mandatory that all dogs must be registered with the city or district council where the owner resides. As a prerequisite, all dogs are classified as dangerous or menacing. All dogs must be micro-chipped, and fees for registration differ between councils. The same prerequisites apply across New Zealand:

- All dogs over 12 weeks old are required to be registered
- The registration tag must be attached to a collar that must be worn permanently around your dog's neck

- Registrations must be renewed annually
- The colour of the tag changes every year for easy identification of expired tags
- Discounts are offered for veterinary proof that a dog has been spayed or neutered
- Fees for working dogs (herding, police, etc.) are discounted
- Service dogs such as guide dogs for the blind or disabled are mostly registered free of charge

Failure to licence a dog or renew a licence a can result in a fine.

f) South Africa

Dog licenses were abolished in various cities and provinces in South Africa over a period of time. The final abolishment was in 2013. Although micro-chipping is not mandatory, any dog obtained through a rescue shelter must be micro-chipped as well as spayed or neutered before the adoption can proceed. Rescue shelters in South Africa will not negotiate on those rules.

Also, the Kennel Union of South Africa (the only all-breed registry) has made it mandatory that all breeding dogs must be micro-chipped to be registered and breeders must abide by these responsibilities.

g) The United States of America

Most states, municipalities or other jurisdictions require dog licences.

Prerequisites and fees are set by individual jurisdictions. In most cases, the licence is only issued on veterinary proof that the dog has been vaccinated against rabies and the license is only valid until the next vaccination is required.

Some jurisdictions offer discounts on licence fees where provide veterinary proof is provided that a dog has been spayed or neutered.

Micro-chipping is not mandatory.

Failure to renew a licence in jurisdictions that require dog licenses can result in a fine.

2. The Price of a Goldendoodle

With the rise in popularity of Goldendoodles as household pets, many sellers have inflated their prices. In some countries, their popularity has led to sellers having waiting lists and accepting deposits for unborn puppies ranging from $50 to $250 or £40 to £190. In some instances deposits are non-refundable should you change your mind or anything untoward happen before birthing.

a) Breeders

You can expect to pay the following for a Goldendoodle puppy bought from a breeder:

Standard F1 23+ Kilograms or 50 Pounds and above	$ 950 to $1,500 £ 722 to £1,139
Medium F1 20± Kilograms or 40 to 50 Pounds	$1,250 to $1,800 £950 to £1,367
Small F1 9± Kilograms or 15 to 30 Pounds	$1,600 to $2,000 £1,215 to £1,519

The breeders' term 'F1' in Chapter 5 under 'Breeders'.

b) Pet Stores and Online

The prices for Goldendoodles advertised online range from $660 to $1,310 or £500 to £995. Although much cheaper than the prices charged by breeders, there is no guarantee offered and no vaccinations that come with the purchase.

3. Necessities and Accessories

There are some necessities that you will have to buy for your Goldendoodle even if it is going to be living inside your house (which it must do).

Allowing your Goldendoodle to sit on the furniture and sleep in peoples' beds is a decision that must be made upfront, even before you bring your Goldendoodle home. As a puppy, it will naturally want to follow you wherever you go, and if you don't want it on any of your furniture, you must start to train it immediately to understand that all furniture is a no-go zone.

If your furniture is a no-go zone, you have to have somewhere else to place your puppy when you are sitting or sleeping. A nice soft, cosy dog bed with a soft blanket or two will be ideal. You can put the dog bed close to you so that the puppy will still feel safe and comfortable.

If you decide to allow your Goldendoodle the full run of the house, a few washable throws will be ideal to put over furniture you want to protect from muddy paws and the regular paw-licking routine.

Also, your Goldendoodle will need a feeding bowl and water bowls relative to its size and a grooming set, dog chews and toys.

a) Dog Beds

Choose a dog bed that will comfortably fit your Goldendoodle when it is fully-grown and not one that fits it as a puppy. Healthy puppies grow extremely fast, and within six months they have reached their approximate adult height. There is still a lot of setting out to do as muscles and bones develop over the months to come, but you don't want to buy a bed that is too small and has to be replaced within a few months.

It is a good idea to have two dog beds - one for indoors and one for outdoors. The outdoor bed should be more hardwearing in composition.

Dog beds come in all shapes and sizes, some raised from the floor on a low platform, others with a basket outer and others made completely of fabric. None are better than the other, its matter of personal choice. There are however a few practicalities to bear in mind. The dog bed you choose:

- Must be easily washable
- Must be thick and soft on the inside
- Must be comfortable and offer adequate padding
- Must not be very heavy making it difficult to move around
- The fabric must be durable so that it won't easily tear
- The stuffing must be even giving the bed a sturdy feel

All un-neutered and some neutered male dogs will scent-mark what they regard to be theirs. A dog bed is an obvious item that will be scent-marked. If you are going to select a male Goldendoodle it is vital to ensure that the outer of the bed is durable and washable; made of a tough non-absorbent fabric that repels water similar to canvas.

Dog beds are readily available from pet stores, retail stores, and vets' consulting rooms as well as online.

Depending on the size of your Goldendoodle you would be looking to buy a small, medium or large bed. For a good quality bed (with dogs quality definitely lasts longer) you can expect to pay $20 to $50 or £15 to £38.

b) Blankets

Your Goldendoodle will be happy with any soft, warm and comfortable blanket. You would need at least three blankets - one to line its dog bed, and two to cover your Goldendoodle. Remember, dogs feel the cold just as humans do. Some are more inclined to feel cold than others.

Keep an eye on your Goldendoodle in colder months to see if you need to add another blanket, or replace thin blankets with thicker ones.

You can, of course, buy fancily printed dog blankets, but it is not necessary. Almost every household has one or two spare blankets, and those will do very well. If you have a large blanket, you can cut it in two and either save the one half or use both halves to make up two blankets.

It's a fact that all dogs, including Goldendoodles, hide their toys and chews in their bedding and then gnaw through the blankets to get to their hidden treasure. No dog is the proud owner of blankets that do not have holes in them unless you have just put new blankets down.

All dogs also drag their blankets around, especially when they are still puppies and your Goldendoodle will be no different.

Blankets have to be washed regularly because they are part of a dog's play and buying expensive 'dog-blankets' is a waste of money!

c) Feeding and Water Bowls

As with a dog bed, remember that your Goldendoodle puppy will grow much bigger very fast so choose a feeding bowl that will be suitable when it has reached its adult size.

Don't waste money on puppy bowls. When you first bring your puppy home, you can feed it in a heavy ceramic bowl or dish and keep water in a deeper, heavy ceramic or stainless steel bowl. Always remove the food bowl once your puppy has finished eating.

Avoid the temptation to use plastic dishes. Don't buy anything plastic at all for your Goldendoodle (and preferably not for yourself either). Many plastics contain toxins that are harmful to animals and humans. Plastic waste clogs up landfills because it does not break-down completely, it contaminates our oceans and plastic pollution is destroying many eco-systems.

Buying a Goldendoodle a plastic feeding or water bowl is a recipe for disaster. The plastic bowl will most definitely be chewed, your dog will ingest potentially toxic and indigestible plastic, and that could cost you an expensive visit to the vet, and you will have to buy a new feeding or water bowl!

Always buy high quality feeding bowls. Stainless steel is the best option, and the bowls will last for your Goldendoodles entire lifetime and beyond. Make sure that the water bowls that you buy are bigger than the feeding bowls because the water bowls must be left out permanently and you don't want the water bowls to empty too quickly. Buy two water bowls, one for outdoors and one for indoors.

Also, ensure that the stainless steel bowls that you buy are of the non-tip type that has a solid outer section that extends outwards making the bottom circumference of the bowl wider than the top circumference.

Depending on the size of your Goldendoodle you would be looking to buy a small, medium or large feeding bowl and two medium or large water bowls.

For good quality, non-tip stainless steel water and feeding bowls you can expect to pay between $10 and $20 or £8 to £15 each.

d) Chews and Toys

Dog chews and toys are an essential and ongoing purchase, especially while your Goldendoodle is a puppy. If you do not provide your Goldendoodle with a variety of chews and toys, it won't be long before your shoes, furniture and other household and garden items become your Goldendoodle's entertainment.

Always ensure that the chews and toys that you give your Goldendoodle are safe for dogs. Safe-for-dogs means that the chew or toy is not made of plastic, does not contain chemical toxins and cannot shatter or splinter into sharp pieces, that will not only cut your Goldendoodles mouth inside but if ingested could cut into the tissue of the oesophagus and stomach lining. If the oesophagus or stomach lining are cut and begin to bleed, your Goldendoodle could bleed to death in a matter of minutes depending on how deep the cut is. Even a small cut in the digestive system can lead to fatal blood loss. If you suspect that your Goldendoodle has ingested a sharp object, take it to the vet immediately.

For large and medium Goldendoodles, choose chews and toys that are quite big and robust. For a small Goldendoodle, opt for smaller chews and toys that it can play with comfortably.

Chews don't last and have to be replaced every few weeks or months, depending on the type. Hooves can last for a few months (depending on the chewing capacity of your Goldendoodle) and hide chews will last for a few weeks. A note of caution on hoof chews, if your Goldendoodle is an aggressive chewer and has jaws strong enough to break off large pieces of hoof it is best to take the hooves away and not buy anymore. Large sharp pieces of the hoof can be dangerous to the digestive system, and they are indigestible if swallowed. Although they are unlikely to do any serious harm, they could cause vomiting because they are indigestible.

Always opt for natural chews and not commercially manufactured chews. Keep away from brightly coloured hide products that are coloured with dyes. There is no valid reason to dye any natural dog chew other than to make the product look 'attractive'. A dog chew that looks 'attractive' is purely for human appeal and serves the dog no purpose.

For a pack of natural, chemical free hide chews you can expect to pay between $14to $20 or £10 to £16. Each pack contains any number of pieces, ranging from about 4 (huge) to 20 (small) pieces depending on the size of the dog.

For a pack of animal hooves or horn pieces, you can expect to pay between $14 to $20 or £10 to £16 for a pack of 6 pieces. One pack should last for quite a few months.

Both hide chews, animal hooves and horn pieces are a source of protein for your Goldendoodle and maintain dental hygiene.

As an added stimulation for your Goldendoodle when chewing on a hoof or horn, you can freeze some broth in a hoof or horn, or put some peanut butter into either, ensuring that you get the peanut butter right down to the bottom. That's a sure winner to keep your Goldendoodle occupied.

When choosing toys for your Goldendoodle, avoid plastic toys! Also avoid standard tennis balls, particularly while your Goldendoodle is a puppy. Many dogs gnaw the furry coating off the tennis balls and ingest it. It is not a natural substance, and although it may not cause any serious health issues, it can cause vomiting because it is indigestible.

For medium and small Goldendoodle puppies an empty toilet roll or kitchen towel holder can make an entertaining toy as they roll it around and chew on it. If the puppy shreds the cardboard holder and leaves the pieces lying around, they have a great toy to play with that will cost you nothing. If the puppy shreds the cardboard holder and swallows the pieces, it is best that you stop giving them to your puppy. Cardboard offers no nutrition but fills the puppy's the stomach leaving less space for healthy food. If your puppy ingests too much cardboard it can become constipated.

The best toys for your Goldendoodle are rope toys and stuffed toys. Some dogs will almost immediately rip a stuffed toy open and pull out the stuffing if the outer fabric is not very durable. It doesn't matter because they will continue playing with 'empty' toy. If this happens, it is essential that you pick up all the stuffing and take it away from your dog before it swallows some of it.

Rope toys can be bought individually or in packs, which are more cost-effective. Packs are specifically made-up for small, medium and large dogs.

You can expect to pay between $15 to $20 or £11 to £16 for a pack of various rope chews. Individual stuffed toys range from $6 to $10 or £5 to £8 depending on the size.

e) Crates, Collars and Leads

If you are taking your Goldendoodle for a ride in your vehicle for any reason, it is best put in a crate, not only for its sake but yours as well. Crating protects your Goldendoodle in the event of a motor accident and a curious dog roaming around in a vehicle can distract the driver and potentially lead to an accident.

Crates are available in various sizes and constructed to hold different dog weights, which is particularly important if you own a Large Goldendoodle.

You can buy soft crates made of a nylon/canvas fabric with mesh sides, plastic crates (which are best avoided) and wire crates.

Before you buy a crate, it is very important that you measure your Goldendoodle's height (from foot to shoulder) and length (from nose to tail). If your Goldendoodle is still a puppy, you will have to estimate its adult height and length, adding a little to ensure that it will fit comfortably in its crate later on.

Some crates come with a soft, washable mattress included and others not. If the crate that you choose does not come with a mattress, it is vital that you buy one separately. Not only will it be unpleasant for your Goldendoodle to sit on a cold surface while travelling, but a mattress prevents your Goldendoodle from sliding back and forth with the motion of the vehicle.

Goldendoodles need to be walked daily if you don't have a very large property that allows them to get enough exercise from running and play.

It is mandatory in most countries that dogs walked in public places must be on a lead and can only be allowed to walk freely in designated areas.

If you buy a good quality lead, it will last for years. Cheap leads are often not very strong and wear through. If you notice it is worn through before you and your Goldendoodle leave home, it won't be an issue, but if it snaps while you are walking it could result in your Goldendoodle getting lost. If you are not able to find your Goldendoodle quickly enough and it can't find its way home, your Goldendoodle could end up being picked up as a stray or worse.

A lead needs a collar to attact to, and although most collars are adjustable, it must fit your Goldendoodle comfortably. You will have to buy at least two collars in the first year of your Goldendoodles life. One for when it's a puppy and another for when it gets bigger. The rule of thumb with dog collars is that you must be able to comfortably fit two fingers between the collar and your Goldendoodle's neck.

Crates

A fabric crate will cost you between $20 to $30 or £15 to £23 depending on the size you choose. Most fabric crates come fitted with a removable padded mattress. Fabric crates and mattresses are fully machine-washable. They are also unlikely to cause your Goldendoodle any injury if it becomes panicked in the crate for any reason.

A plastic crate will cost you between $25 to $30 or £19 to £23 depending on the size you choose. They do not come with a padded mattress. A mattress will cost you anywhere between $9 to $30 or £7 to £23 depending on the size and quality you choose. Bear in mind that the mattress must fit snugly in the crate from back corners to front corners. If it does not, your Goldendoodle will still slide around the crate with the motion of the vehicle.

Collars

Dog collars are made of leather with a typical buckle or of nylon with a plastic snap closing mechanism. Most collars are adjustable, but you must still consider how much growing your Goldendoodle will be doing over the next few months when you select a collar.

Both leather and nylon collars are equally strong if they are well made. Choose quality and ensure that the link on the collar that will hold the lead is strong and unlikely to snap. Dog collars come in a range only limited by your imagination. They offer all colours, colour combinations, designs and prints conceivable. The choice is yours!

You can expect to pay anywhere between $5 to $30 or £4 to £23 depending on the collar size, style and embellishments that you choose.

Leads

Dog leads or leashes come in a wide range of styles and lengths and are made of leather or nylon. Both leather and nylon leads are equally strong if they are well made. Choose quality and ensure that the link on the lead that clips on to the collar is strong and unlikely to snap.

You can also get nylon leads that have a slip-loop that does not require a collar to be fitted. The loop is adjustable, and many people use it as a training collar before fitting their dog with a separate collar.

Unless you live in a country where it is mandatory for dogs to wear collars permanently to display their license discs, you need not leave your Goldendoodles collar on permanently, and a slip-loop lead might suit you better when going for walks.

Some leads are extendable, with some extending for up to 70 meters or 200 feet. Obviously, such long leads are not intended for walks around the suburbs and are best suited to outdoor adventure trips, picnics, etc. You can expect to pay anywhere between $6 to $30 or £5 to £23 depending on the type and length of lead that you choose.

f) Dog Kennels

If you do not have an enclosed area outside that is sheltered from the sun, rain and snow where your Goldendoodle rests, you will have to buy a good quality dog kennel in a size that will comfortably fit your Goldendoodle.

Although you can buy outside dog kennels made from plastic and metal, wooden kennels are the best option. Wood is a natural product that allows for good ventilation, and if the wood panels are interlocked and treated on the outside to resist water, wood is by far the best option.

Outside dog kennels made from plastic have only one entrance/exit and ventilation inside the kennel is almost non-existent. They tend to become very hot inside in warm weather and offer little insulation in cold weather. The only positive feature of a plastic kennel in that it is waterproof.

Metal kennels also have very poor ventilation and can become extremely hot in warm weather and ice-cold in cold weather. Depending on the construction, they are often not waterproof and they are prone to rust.

You must choose a kennel that stays dry inside, is well ventilated and well insulated to be cool inside in warm weather and warm inside in cold weather. The kennel must be elevated from the ground to prevent water running in and damp building up. There must also be a comfortable padded mattress inside.

You can expect to pay anywhere from $200 to $500 or £150 to £380 depending on the size and type of outdoor kennel you choose. These price estimates are based on quality, durable outdoor kennels. Only choose a kennel for your Goldendoodle that you would be willing to live in yourself if you had to. If an outdoor kennel is unfit for you, it is unfit for your Goldendoodle!

g) Veterinary Costs

Veterinary costs vary from one veterinary practice to another and from country to country. There are no set standards for veterinary fees, and a consultation fee only can range from $50 to $110 or £38 to £85 depending on the practice. The cost of each vaccine ranges from$10 to $30 or £8 to £23 over and above.

Puppies generally require three sets of vaccinations in their first year although some vets do the vaccinations in two rounds. An annual booster vaccination is required from thereon.

Treatment of any gastric conditions can cost on average an additional $660 or £500 and a skin condition $330 or £250. It is very difficult to forecast what you would have to pay in vets bills for your Goldendoodle because any dog could have latent health conditions or get injured and require veterinary care. Buying a Goldendoodle puppy from an ethical and reputable breeder may cost you more initially, but it could save you from vet's bills in the long-run. The opposite could be true as well. You could buy a Goldendoodle puppy online or from a pet store and have a happy, healthy puppy that grows into a happy, healthy adult dog.

Taking out pet medical insurance is an option, but the lower the premium, the lower the annual claim thresholds. Premiums start at about $5 or £4 per month up to $100 or £76 per month, but you must read the terms and conditions very carefully before you sign-up. Pet medical insurance is definitely a case of you get what you pay for, and you could find yourself paying monthly insurance premiums and still having to cover the bulk of the veterinary bills if your Goldendoodle does get very ill or is injured.

h) Conclusion on Costs

It is almost impossible to calculate the cost of keeping a Goldendoodle over a 10 to 15 year period. Prices go up, one Goldendoodle may require more veterinary care than another, and you may choose to send your Goldendoodle to a grooming parlour where another Goldendoodle owner may choose not to. That is why the cost of dog grooming at a grooming parlour hasbeen excluded from this chapter.

Also not included is the cost of dog food and supplements. You may choose to feed your Goldendoodle top-grade dog pellets and tinned meat while another Goldendoodle owner may choose to buy quality raw meat and prepare it together with other homemade food and treats for their Goldendoodle.

There are many recipes for healthy homemade dog food available. The cost there is the time spent cooking and preparing food for your Goldendoodle. There is no right or wrong choice, as long as your Goldendoodle is fed a healthy well-balanced diet.

From reading this chapter, you will learn that responsible Goldendoodle ownership does require a cash investment for up to 15 years. A sizable investment to begin with, and then a more budgetable monthly cost once your Goldendoodle has settled in!

If you cannot afford to pay the money to keep a Goldendoodle, walk away! Owning a pet is a privilege and not compulsory. Think about it and make the right decision for yourself and for the Goldendoodle that you might bring home.

Chapter 5. Selecting the Right Goldendoodle

Goldendoodles are, as you've read in previous chapters, active intelligent dogs that can grow into large dogs.

It is vital that you consider the space that you have available for your new Goldendoodle to live and play. Choosing the right size Goldendoodle is very important because a small dog can fit in and be comfortable anywhere, but a large dog is a completely different story.

Large dogs do not only need adequate running and exercise space, but they need ample living room as well. Goldendoodles want to be part of the family, and if they are excluded, it can cause behavioural problems and even depression. If your new Goldendoodle outgrows your house you can't lock it outside; it will not be able to cope!

A large Goldendoodle that is allowed on the furniture can take up an entire sofa. If not allowed on the furniture its dog bed can take up 25% of a small room. Do you have space for a large Goldendoodle?

These are the type of considerations you need to make when deciding on the right Goldendoodle for your household.

Another consideration is, are you keen on the low shedding factor that comes with Goldendoodles? Remember, Goldendoodles are still a recent hybrid breed, and not all puppies have inherited the low shedding gene of the Poodle. Golden Retrievers shed excessively at the change of seasons, and your new Goldendoodle puppy may have inherited that gene.

Careful planning and consideration must go into your selection if you have specific criteria. On the other hand, if you live in a large property in a large house and have no problem with dogs shedding because you are willing to groom them regularly, then your choice is much easier.

1. Buying Choices

As with all household pets, you can buy a Goldendoodle from an ethical and registered breeder, from a pet store, online advert or you can adopt from a shelter.

Your choice of supplier is very much up to you, what your criteria are for wanting a Goldendoodle specifically and what your opinions and personal ethics dictate.

A Goldendoodle puppy bought from a pet store or an online advert must be taken immediately to a vet for a full health check and first vaccinations even before you take it home. Very few backyard breeders and puppy mills have their puppies vaccinated, and pet stores definitely don't!

Sadly, many puppies bought from online adverts or pet stores become very ill and die almost immediately when they arrive at their new home. Shocking as it is to the family who chose the puppy, early puppy deaths is a direct result of the poor breeding and hygiene standards practised by puppy mills, backyard breeders and most pet stores.

Some people see indiscriminate breeding of dogs from their home as a means of making extra money. Very little money or effort is spent on the well being of breeding dogs or their litters.

Puppies bought online mostly come directly from puppy mills and backyard breeders, and most pet stores get their stock from puppy mills and backyard breeders.

Chronic gastric infections and diarrhoea, as well as Canine Parvovirus, take the life of many new puppies before their owners even get to know them. Canine Parvovirus is a highly contagious viral illness that has a poor prognosis, especially in puppies. All dogs should be vaccinated against Canine Parvovirus annually, but unethical breeders are not willing to expend the money because it will minimise their profits. Newborn puppies born to an un-vaccinated mother have a poor immune system, making them very susceptible to Parvovirus.

Puppies bought from online adverts and pet stores are also often infested with fleas, mites, worms and have allergies and skin conditions as a result. These external and internal parasites can be passed onto your other pets and even to humans in some cases. That is why the stop-off at your vet before you bring your new puppy home is essential.

a) Breeders

Ethical and registered breeders should be your first choice if you are a first-time or novice dog owner, or if you are buying a Goldendoodle with specific criteria in mind.

Ethical breeders run an open trade, allowing you to view the mother and often the father as well, and giving you details of the lineage of both. They will also allow you to view the litter shortly after birth in the breeding environment to allow you to make your selection and advise you on what genes each puppy has inherited. You can accept with relative confidence that you have selected a low shedding Goldendoodle if that is what you want.

You will be able to gauge the probable temperament and the adult size of your Goldendoodle puppy with advice from the breeder and from studying the puppies' lineage.

Good breeders who spend a lot of time with their dogs, treat them like family and get to know all of their breeding dogs individually can come up with likely quirks that your Goldendoodle might have like "If he's anything like his father he'll spend his leisure time lying on his back basking in the sun or infront of a warm fire" - and as your Goldendoodle grows into a young adult you could find him doing just that!

Dogs, like humans, have their own personality as well as individual quirks that can be passed on from one generation to the next. That is the value of buying from an ethical and reputable breeder!

Good breeders will offer a guarantee on your Goldendoodle should it become ill or die within the first few months of its life. Guarantees are generally from three to six months. The guarantee excludes accidental death or death through the negligence of the owner.

You will be given a vaccination card recording all vaccinations up until the time of purchase, and told when the next set of vaccinations are due. Vaccinations need not be done at the same vet if you are buying from a breeder that is out of your area. All you need to do it take the vaccination card to your vet.

Both Golden Retrievers and Poodles are genetically predisposed to Hip and Elbow Dysplasia as well as various eye diseases, and Poodles are also genitally predisposed to von Willebrand's Disease (vWD), which is a bleeding disorder. Reputable breeders will have all breeding dogs DNA screened for evidence of any genetic predisposition to diseases before they put them into a breeding program.

Screening for predisposition to Hip and Elbow Dysplasia is done through genetic testing undertaken through the Orthopaedic Foundation for

Animals (OFA) or PennHIP. Both offer an accurate means of testing young dogs to establish their risk of developing Hip or Elbow Dysplasia in later life. A written report is issued and given to the breeder for each dog tested. Only dogs that are certified negative for any orthopaedic disease predisposition should be in a breeding program.

Screening for predisposition to eye disease is done through the Canine Eye Registration Foundation (CERF). Young dogs are genetically tested for predisposition to eye disease at any age. A written report is issued and given to the breeder for each dog tested. Only dogs that are certified negative for any predisposition to eye disease should be in a breeding program.

Poodles considered for breeding are also DNA screened for predisposition to von Willebrand's Disease. A written report is issued for each dog tested and given to the breeder. Only Poodles that are certified negative for any predisposition to von Willebrand's Disease should be in a breeding program.

For a reputable breeder, genetic screening of all dogs that are going to enter their breeding program is standard. It is costly, but an essential part of their ethics and reputation. If you buy a Goldendoodle puppy from a reputable breeder, you will be given a copy of the genetic clearances of both the puppy's mother and father.

Breeders dedicated to building and enhancing the Goldendoodles as a breed follow a breeding pattern created to retain the desirable characteristics of Goldendoodles and uphold the original breed intention and standards.

In brief, the breeding patterns maintain the following trend:

- (F1)-first generation Goldendoodles that are the hybrid offspring of a golden retriever and a standard poodle
- (F1B) - second generation Goldendoodles that are the offspring of an (F1) Goldendoodle and a standard poodle

Through following and maintaining this breeding process, breeders enhance the desirable Poodle traits of a low shedding coat, making Goldendoodles almost hypoallergenic. The breeding process also aims to maximise genetic diversity and build a healthy breed by breeding only dogs that have been excluded from genetic predisposition to certain diseases through DNA testing.

Eventually, by consistently breeding Goldendoodles with Goldendoodles, the characteristics will become sustained. Size, temperament and coat-type will become standardised and inherited health conditions eliminated from the breed. Although the breed is still very recent, multi-generational Goldendoodles already have the most consistent characteristics, and they are the foundation of what breeders intend to become a recognised breed.

b) *Pet Stores*

Pet stores buy their stock from backyard breeders and puppymills. No reputable breeder will sell their puppies to a pet store.

Before choosing a Goldendoodle from a pet store, you must have a good idea of what to look for to ensure that you are buying a Goldendoodle. Also, you must be able to gauge the approximate adult size of a puppy; gauge this from the puppy's paw size, skull and long bone circumference.

Dogs that are going to grow into small dogs will tend to have small paws and a more delicate bone structure. Their skull will be notably smaller than dogs that are going to grow into large dogs. Dogs that are going to grow into large dogs will have large paws, with a more thickly set bone structure.

Unfortunately, without knowing the puppy's lineage, it will be almost impossible to tell if it is going to have a low shedding coat or not. All puppies coats are quite flat when they are born and for the first few weeks of their life, and begin the change as they grow older.

If the puppies look obviously ill and there is diarrhoea in the cage, then that is a big red flag. Report any pet store that keeps puppies in unhygienic conditions and treats puppies cruelly to your local animal anti-cruelty authority without delay with the intention of having them closed down. Denying an obviously ill puppy vet treatment is cruel!

Sometimes puppies that are not very active in their cage have been taken away from their mother too soon, and that is the reason for their lethargy. There are puppymills that remove puppies as young as five weeks old from their mother and sell them saying they are older! Pet store owners should have the knowledge to be able to recognise a puppy that is too young to be separated from its mother, but they are either ignorant or turn a blind eye.

If you are an experienced dog owner, buying a Goldendoodle puppy from a pet store is a gamble, but one that you should be able to handle.

Many people are abhorred by backyard breeders and puppy mills and will do what they can to have them closed down. They are of the opinion that the little puppy in the pet store is an innocent victim of an appalling practice that should not suffer as a result. They will buy the puppy to offer it the loving home that its parents never knew.

Other people refuse to buy puppies that have obviously come from backyard breeders and puppy mills, saying that buying them encourages the practice.

Although true, so is the first opinion. It is a matter of opinion and personal ethics.

c) Online

It is difficult to gauge the age or size of Goldendoodle puppies sold online because unlike breeders' websites they do not give any details of the puppies' date of birth or lineage.

Adverts read along the lines of:

- "Our pet Goldendoodle has just given birth to a letter of beautiful puppies ......"
- "For the cheapest Goldendoodle puppies ......"
- "We have beautiful Goldendoodle puppies in a range of colours for sale ......"

It is clear that these adverts are back-yard breeders and puppymills!

Online sellers will usually agree to meet you in a car park of some public place to hand the puppy over to you. You pay, they give you the puppy and then leave. You have no idea what the tiny little life that you are holding in your hands actually is or how healthy it is.

Buying a Goldendoodle online is a risk!

d) Adoption

Many Goldendoodles end up in rescue shelters because people who did not understand the breed brought them home. If you do not understand the Goldendoodle history, you could end up with a dog that you can't handle and that can grow to be a big dog.

It is the Goldendoodle that will pay the price and end up in a rescue shelter.

Many rescues will never be adopted, and unless they are at a no-kill shelter, euthanasia is inevitable. Pretty rough for an innocent life that relied on human beings for love, comfort and its very survival!

Most rescue shelters do their utmost to get dogs adopted. If you are willing to adopt a Goldendoodle, an Internet search for rescue shelters in your area will be a good start. If the shelters in your area do not have any Goldendoodles, they will more than likely help you to find one. The majority of rescue shelters network extensively and actively work together to get dogs adopted.

Another Internet site to go to is Facebook. There are many dog rescue group pages on Facebook started by private individuals and not rescue shelters. Rescue shelters usually support these pages and vice-versa; they network specific breeds or all breeds of dogs that are up for adoption. They post pictures of the dogs and often a short history is included to give you some idea of it's background.

If you see a Goldendoodle on the pages of one of these groups, but it is in an area that is far from where you are, most groups will avidly keep posting for anyone travelling to your area or close-by. These pages as 'liked' by real dog-lovers so it is usually only a matter of time before a volunteer Goldendoodle-taxi driver steps up and contacts you to make arrangements to meet for the delivery.

All rescue shelters and Facebook groups will expect you to pay for vaccinations and spay/neuter cost if applicable. A home inspection is almost always a pre-requisite as well to ensure that you have adequate space and means to take care of the Goldendoodle you want to adopt.

Don't become defensive when you are asked to approve a home inspection. The reason is valid! Not only has the Goldendoodle been abandoned before, but dog-fighting is rife worldwide. A Goldendoodle with its gentle nature would make a very good bait-dog to train fighting dogs. The minimal fee charged by a rescue shelter or group is nothing in comparison to what dog fighters make in gambling and prize money! A home inspection is a confirmation that you are who you say you are and an act of dedication by rescue centre staff and Facebook page volunteers.

It is seldom that you would get young Goldendoodle puppies from a rescue shelter or online rescue group unless a pregnant female was surrendered or abandoned. In that case, although the mother may be a Goldendoodle the father could be any breed. A point to keep in mind!

You would more likely find a young Goldendoodle of around a year old. That is a common age when dog owners will surrender or abandon a dog. It is mostly owners who have made no effort to research the dog breed or put any effort into seeking professional training to teach themselves and the dog. They will surrender the dog because it 'grew too big' or because it is 'naughty'. Many people fail to recognise intelligence in a dog and mistake it for 'naughtiness'.

Dogs are surrendered or abandoned at any age though, and some are picked up as strays. Many stray dogs get lost accidentally and are sadly not reunited with their owners if they are not micro-chipped. There are also valid and often sad reasons that bring a dog to the door of rescue shelters. Their owner could have passed on, and no family members could keep the dog, or their owners lost their job and are unable to keep the dog, and many people can't afford to keep their dogs anymore due to financial constraints. These are often very tearful sorrowful partings.

There are good reasons to adopt a Goldendoodle rather than buy. These include:

- Adoption is definitely the most affordable option and is much less risky than buying from a pet store or online advert
- To encourage adoptions, rescue shelters and online rescue groups keep their adoption fees low, generally covering only the vet fees, cost of vaccinations and any veterinary treatment or procedures
- They charge a small administration fee to cover their costs but rely mainly on donations from sponsors and supporters
- Unlike a Goldendoodle bought from a pet store or online, an adopted Goldendoodle has already been treated by a vet and they give you the proof
- Adopting an adult dog does have advantages, like some have already been housetrained and have had obedience training
- Other advantages are that as adult dogs, their temperament is already established; most rescue shelters and groups pre-test the dogs for their reaction to other dogs and cats, and also how they react to small children
- They share this information openly, and you will see them networking dogs as 'must be an only dog', 'good with other cats and dogs', 'no small children', 'good with children', etc.

- Adult dogs require less attention, in the longrun, but you may have to give your adopted Goldendoodle some special love and care at first if it has come from a place of neglect
- Goldendoodles are intelligent, affectionate dogs that thrive on human company; abuse and neglect can lead to introversion and fear of humans
- Any dog that has become fearful and introverted through fear of abuse, or from neglect will blossom before your eyes if you show it patience, love and kindness; dogs forgive very easily
- Animal lovers run rescue shelters and groups and they will take time to get to know the dogs in their care; fostering for a short while before being networked for adoption is common to allow a dog to readjust or recover
- As with ethical and reputable breeders, you will be able to discuss a Goldendoodles temperament, behaviour and personality before you make your decision to adopt
- You get to see the Goldendoodle; you know what size it is and if it sheds its coat or has a low-shedding coat
- Lastly, it's an ethical option; it is a privilege to take a Goldendoodle from a past of neglect and suffering and bring it into a warm and loving household where it becomes part of the family.

If you do opt for adoption, you must be understanding with your new Goldendoodle in the early weeks after you bring it home. It will be confused and most likely afraid. Even if it was surrendered from a loving home, it is in a strange place with strange people and strange smells. Before it came to your house it was housed at the rescue shelter or in a foster home; it does not know what to expect next!

Give it time and have patience. Allow your Goldendoodle to get to know you and the family. Don't be offended if it backs off when you want to stroke or give it cuddles. It doesn't know you yet.

For the most part, adopted dogs start to settle in very well after a week, as they adapt to their new surroundings and the daily routines.

There are adopted dogs though who become anxious, depressed or both. Sometimes it can act out on its fear and insecurity by either hiding in some dark corner for most of the day, or by running around and being destructive. Both are reactions to what it is experiencing and are not a long-term reflection of your new Goldendoodles personality.

If your Goldendoodle is hiding away don't drag it out from where it hides and try to force it to interact. That will just increase its anxiety. Visit its safe-place regularly and speak softly to it using its new name often. Don't try to touch it. Reassure it, tell it that it has nothing to fear and then leave without making any attempt to move it away from it's safe-place. Keep doing this and if you are a family encourage all family members to stop by its safe-place regularly to offer love and reassurance.

Slowly your Goldendoodle will emerge, reacting to your gentle kindness. At first, it may stand or sit and watch you from a distance. Acknowledge it but do not attempt to move towards it. Allow it to approach you. It can take quite a few weeks for it to actually come right up to you and allow you to stroke and pet it, but when that happens, it will be a most wonderful experience for both of you. You have won the trust of a dog once betrayed; you will be loved forever by a dog who did not know love!

If your new Goldendoodle is acting out on its anxiety by running around and being destructive, don't chase after it yelling threats, which will make it more anxious. Speak in a firm, but kind voice using its new name often. Don't punish or ignore it. If it approaches you, stroke it and speak softly; try to calm it down so that it can let go of its anxiety and realise that there is nothing to fear. As it lets go of its anxiety and fear, the destructive behaviour should stop.

Make sure that you have lots of dog chews and toys to keep your newly adopted Goldendoodle occupied. Take it for walks, speak to it regularly and make it part of the family and household routines.

Many adopted dogs turn out to be rough diamonds. With love and kindness, they shine with a most beautiful resonance. They become the most loving, adorable household pets that will reward you with unconditional love and loyalty into eternity.

Chapter 6. Preparing your Home for a New Puppy

You have done the research, made your decisions and you are ready to bring your new Goldendoodle puppy home.

Before the 'big-day' there are a couple of checks and balances that you have to do to ensure that there are no calamities when the puppy arrives.

Often when you do a lot of planning and preparation, some of the obvious matters are overlooked.

Basic Requirements

a) Is your Outside Yard Puppy-Proofed Everywhere?

Puppies are small, and even a large-sized Goldendoodle puppy is small. Puppies might not have built up physical strength yet, but they are very supple and can fit through bars, under fences and hedges and crawl into small places like water drainage outlets, etc.

You have to puppy-proof your yard! Check for any gaps in fencing or hedges, wind string between bars and place wire mesh over drainage outlets. If you have a swimming pool or pond, it should be secured or completely covered so that the puppy can't reach it. Goldendoodles are innately good swimmers, but a puppy's muscles are undeveloped. If it falls into water that is deeper than it can step out of, it will have to swim. The swimming will tire it out quickly, and it can drown. A small puppy is best kept away from deep water until it grows stronger!

Puppies grow very quickly so you can remove a lot of the things that you put up or closed off in a few months.

b) Is your House Puppy-Proofed Everywhere?

You have to puppy-proof your house! Remove all chewable items that are within your puppy's reach. It's best to place toilet rolls on top of the cistern and not on the holder for a few months while your puppy settles in and starts puppy training. Most puppies love rolling toilet paper from the roll on a holder and then shredding it to pieces. The same applies to books, newspapers and magazines. Keep them well out of reach!

Are you in the habit of taking your shoes and socks off and leaving them wherever? Get out of that habit fast! Dogs love worn sweaty shoes and socks because your scent is very strong on them. Your Goldendoodle puppy will indulge in chewing your shoes and socks if you don't pack your shoes away and put your socks in the washing.

c) Are you Ready to Feed your Baby Goldendoodle?

Have you bought or prepared enough puppy food and do you have feeding and water bowls? Have you got enough dog chews and biscuits? If you don't have chews and biscuits, your baby Goldendoodle will soon be chewing your shoes and furniture.

d) Is your Baby Goldendoodle's Bed and Blankets Ready?

By now you have already decided whether your Goldendoodle will be allowed on your furniture or to sleep in your bed, apply the rule from day one!

If you are not going to allow your Goldendoodle on your furniture, it is vital that you have a soft, warm bed for it that you can keep close to where you are sitting. When you go to bed, you can bring your Goldendoodle's bed into your bedroom and place it near your bed so that it does not feel alone.

e) Have you Stockpiled Newspaper and Paper Towels?

Remember, your Goldendoodle puppy is a baby. It does not have full control of its balder and rectal muscles just like a human baby. In the early weeks, if it has to go it has to go! You cannot punish it; it's a baby. Just clean up and persevere with house training. Your Goldendoodles muscles will strengthen and at the same time it will begin to understand house training and toilet rules.

Chapter 7. Bringing your New Puppy Home

At last the day has arrived! You are bringing your new Goldendoodle puppy home. Excitement from all the humans in the house, but total confusion for your new Goldendoodle!

Don't be disappointed if your new puppy seems confused and more inclined to want to hide from you than want to play with you. Very young puppies don't play very much, they sleep mostly, and too much activity can be intimidating.

1. Remember that a Puppy is a Baby

In their excitement to get to know their new puppy, many people lose sight of the fact that a puppy is a baby. Like a human baby, a puppy is unable to process what is happening. Its mind is underdeveloped and immature.

If you bought it from a breeder, it has just been separated from its mother and litter mates. It has been taken from the only environment it has ever known and is now in unfamiliar surroundings. Dogs identify things by smell and scent, so all the smells are unfamiliar as well. Puppies kept with their mothers for up to 12 weeks have formed a strong bond with her. Your puppy may cry and pine for its mother for quite a few days before it begins to settle.

Give it lots of love and cuddles and allow it to sleep in the same room that you are in so that it can become accustomed to your voice and scent. If you are watching television, let it sleep in your living room. If you are outdoors, let it sleep outdoors near to where you are but away from cold draughts or direct sun. If you have gone to bed, let it sleep in your bedroom.

If you bought your Goldendoodle puppy from a pet store or online, it may not only be confused because it is in unfamiliar surroundings, but it may be unfamiliar with human contact. The breeding conditions in puppy mills are mostly horrendous with little attention paid to any of the dogs, including new-born puppies. Often human contact is minimal with breeding quarters being hosed clean from a distance, water bowls filled with a hosepipe and food dropped into breeding enclosures via a funnel that leads to the feeding bowls (if there are any).

If you can see that your new puppy is afraid of human contact, don't fear. After a few days of love and cuddles, it will become used to you very quickly. Animals, just like humans, respond well to genuine love and kindness.

Because puppies are still babies, your little Goldendoodle might sleep much more than you expected. In the early weeks of their life puppies spend most of their time sleeping. Children could find this very disappointing if they waited excitedly for the puppy to come home. Explain to them that they must not try to awaken it; it must sleep to grow big and strong.

Their routine is not un-similar to human babies. They sleep, wake up, cry for food, you feed them, they must be carried to the designated toilet area quite quickly after eating, they play for about 15 to 20 minutes and then flop down wherever they are at the moment and fall fast asleep.

You should feed your baby Goldendoodle four small meals a day. The amount of food given at each meal will depend on its size; the larger the puppy, the bigger the meal portion. Your vet should be able to advise you, or you can read the feeding guide on commercial puppy food packs. The measurement is per the puppy's weight. Remember, puppies must be fed puppy food that is highly nutritious and easily digestible. Quality commercially made puppy food is best in the first few months of your puppy's life to ensure it gets all the nutrients it needs.

Reduce the number of meals and increase the meal portion size as your Goldendoodle puppy becomes more active and stays awake for longer periods of time. There is no right age to move a dog from puppy food to adult dog food - it depends on the dog. As its age becomes measured in months rather than weeks, you can begin feeding your young Goldendoodle adult dog food. If it seems to have difficulty chewing or digesting it, go back to puppy food for a while longer and then try the adult food again.

Feed an adult dog two meals a day. Once your tiny Goldendoodle has become a gangly teen, you can probably feed it adult food twice a day. For dogs of all ages, it is best to keep to a routine and feed it at the same time each morning and evening. All dogs are creatures of habit, and they thrive on routine. It won't be long before your Goldendoodle begins reminding you that it's almost breakfast time or dinner time. Many dogs will stand at the cupboard door where their food is, or if they can reach it bring you their food bowl.

Fresh, clean water must be available to your Goldendoodle puppy 24 hours a day. Change water daily and wash the bowls out regularly, particularly in warm weather to prevent the growth of water-borne bacteria and algae. If there are signs of algae build up in the water bowls, you get rid of these by wiping the empty bowls with a swab soaked in white vinegar. Rinse the bowls well afterwards.

2. Socializing your New Puppy

Because puppies are babies, they have to be taught how you want them to behave and how to interact with other members of the family, including canine, feline and feathered family members as well.

It is always best to introduce your new Goldendoodle to members of the household almost immediately. At this stage you must be more aware of the reaction of existing family members than that of your Goldendoodle puppy.

Closely supervise children when they are handling the new puppy. Caution them against over-enthusiasm, and guide them on how to hold the puppy. Explain to them that the new little Goldendoodle is a still a baby.

When introducing your little Goldendoodle to canine, feline or feathered family members, it is best that you hold the puppy securely at a distance so that you can remove the puppy very quickly if they react aggressively. Even if they approach the puppy to smell it and look at it, keep holding it in your hands and don't put it down. An aggressive attack can happen very suddenly. Remember, to other household pets this is an intruder.

If there is any sign of aggression from any of your existing pets, keep the puppy at a distance from them but don't remove it completely from their presence. Female cats and dogs often react from their maternal instinct and will be very curious and become attached to the puppy very easily. Male cats and dogs can be completely put off and will flee the scene very quickly. Large birds like parrots may react with aggression if they feel threatened, but mostly not.

Once the puppy grows bigger and is more inclined to interact with other household pets, you will find that they will be regarded in a different light and bonds soon form. Goldendoodles are known to get on well with all other household pets because they are not innately aggressive.

Even if bonds of play are not formed, you can find that there are unspoken terms of agreement between your new Goldendoodle and other household pets. "If I'm on this side of the room, you stay on the otherside." or "If I'm lying by the fireside you get under a blanket." - type rules. They are real and they exist between household pets worldwide. The most amazing part is that they happen without human intervention. Animals do communicate with each other.

3. Early Puppy Training

Like babies and toddlers, puppies have a short span of attention. You can start with very basic commands from about 8 weeks, but don't expect that your Goldendoodle puppy is going to be a genius!

At this young age and for the next few months you can introduce basic routines and behaviour, but results will be quite poor. You have to have patience. You are dealing with a baby, but at least you are getting your Goldendoodle accustomed to a training routine.

The training routine should not be formal and no specific amount of time should be set aside daily to train your Goldendoodle. Early training is opportunistic! If your puppy is in the right place and is focused, do a bit of training. If it loses interest, let it go.

One of the first training routines introduced is housetraining, and that should start from the first day you bring your puppy home. Although it is pointless because young puppies have very little muscle control over their bladder and rectal muscles, it is vital, and it must become routine for both you.

Everytime your little Goldendoodle wakes up you need to scoop it up and take it to your designated 'toilet' area. It won't walk there by itself at this age. The 'toilet' can be newspaper placed on the same spot in the house, or outside on the grass. All young puppies will wee almost immediately when they wake up. Poop is optional, but not out of the picture so stay with your puppy for a few minutes after it's wee'd. Once it's done, praise your puppy.

The same routine applies after your puppy has finished a meal. Within 5 to 10 minutes after finishing a meal, your puppy will have both a wee and poop. It is part of the natural peristalsis process. As soon as food enters the mouth, an involuntary process is sparked by the brain causing involuntary muscle contractions that move the food from the mouth, through the throat and digestive tract. Any post-digestion waste from the previous meal will be lying in the rectal area, and the process of peristalsis automatically expels it as poop. As your puppy gets older its rectal muscles will strengthen, and it will have more control over its expulsion of digestive waste.

Remember, you must always praise your puppy once it's done in the designated toilet area.

Other basic commands like 'sit' and 'stay' can be introduced at this stage, but again the results will not be great. Sit and stay commands can be given if the opportunity arises. The opportunity would be that you are aware that your little Goldendoodle is focused on you and you can then give the command. If it sits or stays even for a few seconds, give it praise.

In dog training, voice commands must always be accompanied by hand gestures as well. The tone of your voice is very important; firm, but kind. If the puppy does as told, your 'reward' voice tone should be happy and kind.

There must be a difference in the command and reward voice tone, and these must stay constant through your dog's lifetime. Dogs respond to tone of voice, eye contact and body language. The words and hand gestures that you use must also always stay constant as well to avoid confusing your dog. Goldendoodles are sensitive to aggression, so an aggressive voice tone or hand gestures will work against successfully training your Goldendoodle at any age.

4. Set Rules Early-On, but Gently

Like children, dogs also need to be taught rules and routines. Certain rules must be introduced immediately, like housetraining.

a) On the Furniture or Not?

Another rule that must be introduced early on is if you have decided not to allow your Goldendoodle onto the furniture. It must be gently introduced to your puppy right from the start.

Many people make the mistake of allowing the puppy to walk and play on their furniture when it is tiny and cute. Once it gets bigger and more boisterous, they start tossing the young puppy off the furniture. Talk about

Goldendoodle confusion? For sure! Your Goldendoodle will not understand and could feel hurt by this change of approach.

If your rule is 'no dogs on the furniture', it must be applied from day one, and all family members must apply the same rule. You can carry your puppy and hold it on your lap, but it must not be allowed off your lap onto the furniture. When it falls asleep, you must put it into its dog bed placed close by, and that routine must be followed daily by everyone.

If you want to play with the puppy, you must sit on the floor and play with it until it gets tired. Once you see that it is getting tired, you must put it in its dog bed.

It can be a very difficult rule to apply, especially with a family loving dog like a Goldendoodle. That is why it must be implemented immediately and by everyone in the family.

b) Begging for Food from your Plate

Another early rule must be no begging for food when anyone is eating, or the family are eating together. A well-fed dog will not innately beg for food from people's plates unless someone has been feeding them that way.

If you feed your cute little puppy a little piece of food from your plate, it will associate you eating with it getting small treats. It is cute behaviour as a puppy but can become a very annoying habit when your Goldendoodle gets older, and it sits and watches you eat, waiting for a treat. Worse still, it will also sit and watch your dinner guests eating, waiting for a treat from them.

If your Goldendoodle begs for food at human's meal time, it is your fault! You allowed it to associate people eating with being fed treats. It is you and your family who need this training, not your Goldendoodle. The family rule must stand firm 'no feeding the puppy off our plates, ever!'

5. Puppies and Children

It is vital that children are taught from a very early age that all animals are sentient beings that can feel pain (physical and emotional), fear, joy, sadness, depression, etc. – just like human beings.

One of the easiest ways to explain this to children is to tell them to look into an animal's eyes and see they their eyes connect with ours, just like other peoples' do. Toys and other inanimate objects don't connect with people in the same manner. That means that animals are not toys! All children must be taught to treat all animals with respect and kindness.

Always supervise children when they are handling the puppy. If very small children want to hold the new puppy, it must be done with an adults' hands only a fraction away to remove the puppy if the child is holding it too tightly or too loosely. Too tightly can cause the puppy pain, discomfort or even suffocation; too loosely can let the puppy fall.

Even older children must understand clearly that puppies must not be carried like a human baby, lying on their back and rocked back and forth. It is unnatural for a young puppy to be carried on its back and if it has just eaten, it can cause it to vomit.

Many older dogs, however, love being cradled like a baby, but only if the dog is comfortable with it and when it's much older.

If you have adopted an adult Goldendoodle, explain to your children that it will feel strange at first, so it probably won't want to play with them immediately. Put them in the Goldendoodles shoes - when they just started school or went to day care on their own. Do they remember how they felt? They were unsure and didn't really know what to do. Explain to them that that is how your adopted Goldendoodle feels. Then take your children back to their experience after a few days at school or day care, what happened? They had made friends and didn't feel strange anymore. Once your adopted Goldendoodle has settled, it will feel the same, and they will be its's, new friends.

Chapter 8. Day-to-Day Care

Goldendoodles are not high maintenance dogs when it comes to day-to-day care. They need to be fed a healthy diet, have adequate physical exercise, be stimulated mentally by human interaction and play and get a lot of love by being made part of your household. Apart from a few other requirements, that's pretty much it!

1. Clipping and Grooming

Whether your Goldendoodle has inherited the shedding coat of the Golden Retriever or the low-shedding coat of the Poodle, it will have to be brushed at least twice a week to get rid of dead hair.

If your Goldendoodle sheds, then regular brushing means less hair around your house and in your vehicle. If your Goldendoodle is low shedding, regular brushing removes dead hair entangled in the coat and prevents matting.

Both shedding and low shedding coats should be clipped around the legs and underbelly to prevent its coat becoming entangled in the undergrowth and picking up dead bits of plant material and parasites.

If your Goldendoodle does not have some rough ground to walk on daily to wear its toenails down, they could also need regular clipping. If you don't know how to clip a dog's toenails, it is best you have it done by a vet or at a grooming parlour. If you cut into the nail-bed it will be extremely painful for your Goldendoodle; the cut bloodvessels will bleed and can even become infected.

If your Goldendoodle's nails are left to grow too long, it can become painful for it to walk. In extreme cases of overgrown nails, the nail can grow in towards the paw pads and eventually cut into the flesh of the paw pad.

If you choose, you can send your Goldendoodle to a dog parlour every six weeks or so for a bath, clipping and to have its nails trimmed.

2. Bathing

Goldendoodles need only be bathed every six weeks or so unless they have become really muddy or rolled in something unpleasant.

Because Goldendoodles lineage is from water-dogs, their coat contains oils that protect their skin from getting wet and also make their coat water repellent. Bathing them too regularly will wash away these oils and negatively affect their coat condition.

What is very important though is to wipe the inside of your Goldendoodle's ears out at least twice a week. They are prone to ear infections and keeping the inside of their ears clean and dry can aid to prevent infection.

Wipe the inside of both ears gently but thoroughly with a soft, warm damp cloth to remove any dirt or potential bacteria that may be in the ears. A drop of teatree oil can be added to a basin of warm water before you steep your cloth. Wring the cloth out well before you wipe your Goldendoodle's ears. After wiping with a damp cloth, dry each ear thoroughly with an absorbent towel or soft piece of paper towel.

If while wiping your Goldendoodles ears out you notice any inflammation or bad odour in any ear, a visit to the vet will be required as ear infections can spread quickly into the inner ear.

Although a course of antibiotics may be needed initially, your vet will most likely give you eardrops and topical antibacterial cream that can be used in the future as soon as you notice any signs of infection.

If your Goldendoodle loves swimming, its ears must be cleaned and dried everytime after a swim. Because of the way Goldendoodles ears hang down, there is little ventilation and water in the ears is unlikely to evaporate. The warmth and dampness in the ear will make it a perfect breeding place for bacteria.

3. Full Body Inspection

A full body inspection of your Goldendoodle should become a standard routine when it is still a young puppy so that it will become accustomed to it.

You can do it while you are brushing it. Rub your fingers up under its coat to feel for any scabs, lumps or inflammation. You may not feel the inflammation, but your Goldendoodle will flinch or pull away when your fingers rub over the inflamed area.

Part the coat to investigate anything that you find. If it looks concerning it is always better to err on the side of caution and take your Goldendoodle to your vet.

Also, feel your Goldendoodle's body over from nose to tail, applying gentle pressure. If it winces or pulls away, examine the area of the body well for swelling or inflammation. It is important that you begin the full body inspection when your Goldendoodle is still a young puppy because most dogs that are unaccustomed to the routine will not allow you to do it.

Goldendoodles can be genetically predisposed to Hip and Elbow Dysplasia. If your Goldendoodle has developed Hip or Elbow Dysplasia the joint will become sensitive causing it to wince or pull away. The condition is treatable, so the sooner it is diagnosed, the easier it will be to treat.

Another part of your inspection is to look your Goldendoodle straight in the eyes. You are looking for any abnormality in shape of one or both eyes, and opaqueness, dilation or constriction of one or both pupils and any inflammation. Goldendoodles are also genetically predisposed to eye disease that can lead to blindness. Not all eye diseases are treatable, but early diagnosis can allow for treatment that will slow the degeneration of your Goldendoodles eyesight down.

Finally, you should check your Goldendoodle's teeth by lifting the lips to expose the bottom and upper teeth. If you see any inflammation on the gums or any broken or discoloured teeth, your Goldendoodle could have tooth abscess and need dental treatment from your vet. Regular tooth-brushing is recommended; preferably daily. Brushing teeth is definitely best started as young as possible. Most dogs either don't take tooth-brushing well, or will grab the toothbrush and run thinking it a game. Brushing your Goldendoodles teeth every day will require patience and practice!

Chapter 9. Training as your Puppy Grows Older

Most dogs are mature enough to begin serious training for extended periods of time by the age of 6 months. Goldendoodles are very intelligent dogs, so this is definitely the time to begin.

By this age, your Goldendoodle puppy should be quite comfortable with your house training routine as well as basic commands like sit and stay. It should also be much more focused and alert at 6 months.

1. House Training

Most puppies take between 4 to 6 months to house train. If you started training your Goldendoodle puppy from when you first brought it home aged between 8 to 12 weeks, at 6 months of age house training could virtually be done and dusted!

Your puppy should have gained full bladder control at around 16 weeks of age, so by that time, the house training routine should have been sinking into your puppy's mind.

House training a puppy is very straightforward. There is no magic formula, and your puppy will not eventually learn on its own where to go. It requires constant, dedicated patient routine work from you to teach your puppy. Day and night, over and over again!

At 6 months you can still expect your puppy to slip-up occasionally. If your puppy backslides on house training and has some slip-ups at this age it is not cause for alarm. Patience and kind perseverance is key to house training; just keep re-enforcing the routine and remember to praise your puppy when it successfully uses the designated toilet area.

As your puppy grows older you will be able to identify visible signs that it needs to relieve itself. The most common signs are running around in a tight circle, nose to the ground or sudden 'digging' on the spot, nose to the ground. As you get to know your Goldendoodle puppy, you can pick up from its body language when nature calls.

Small-sized dogs sometimes take a bit longer to house train because their bladders are smaller. Also, in warm and hot weather, dogs drink more water, and these factors must be taken into consideration.

The ultimate success of your Goldendoodle's house training is up to you just as much as it is up to your puppy. House training requires disciplined routine from your side. You have to take your puppy to the designated toilet area often, and if nothing happens immediately, you have to stand with your puppy and wait until it happens. Remember to praise your puppy once it has done its business successfully.

If your training routine is not constant and disciplined, you can't blame your puppy if it is taking too long to house train. No dog is un-trainable; if you think your Goldendoodle puppy is un-trainable it is due to human error - yours!8

Your designated toilet area cannot be changed from one place to another until your puppy is completely house trained. If you have opted for an area of newspaper, the puppy will associate newspaper with its toilet routine. If you live in a double storey house, you can have one 'newspaper' area downstairs and one upstairs to save you carrying your Goldendoodle puppy up and down the stairs. If you have opted for an area of grass outside your house, you have to take your puppy out there day and night, through all seasons until it learns to go there on its own. It takes patience and perseverance!

Once your Goldendoodle has been completely house trained things should run smoothly as long as you let it out before bedtime and first thing in the morning. You should not have to stand with it anymore once it knows how the toilet routines work. Always praise it after it has done its business successfully in the right place.

There can still be slip-ups, and they could be stress related (moving to a new house, new baby arriving in the house, divorce, a young adult leaving the house, etc.) Dogs are very sensitive, and they are creatures of habit. They become attached to routines, people and their living environment and any drastic change could cause stress. If this happens, re-focus on housetraining again and give lots of love, reassurance and praise. That should ease your Goldendoodles stress and make it settle again.

Illness would be another reason that makes your Goldendoodle slip-up. Nausea and diarrhoea are quite common because all dogs are inclined to sniff around the garden and find tasty edibles. Unfortunately, sometimes those tasty edibles are not that good and cause a stomach upset. If the diarrhoea is severe you will have to take your Goldendoodle to the vet.

Un-neutered male dogs of all breeds are inclined to scent-mark. The instinct is stronger in some dogs than what it is in others, and no breed is more or less inclined to male scent-marking, particularly if you have more than one male dog. The only way to prevent scent-marking is to have your male dogs neutered. Neutering may not completely stop the scent-marking instinct, but it should curb it considerably.

2. Obedience Training Overview

All dogs are trainable, and there are many different training methods, all of which are successful. Not all training methods suit all dogs' temperament and personality though. The trick is to find a training method that suits you and that works well for your Goldendoodle.

If you are a first-time or novice dog owner, you might prefer to take your Goldendoodle to obedience training classes. There are also many books available that take you through the various stages of dog training.

There are pros and cons for taking your Goldendoodle to obedience training classes. Pros include:

- If you have no idea where to begin training, let a professional dog trainer guide you
- If your Goldendoodle in an only pet, obedience training classes are recommendedd because it exposes your Goldendoodle to other dogs
- If you have tried training but your Goldendoodle regards it as play and doesn't listen to you
- A professional dog trainer can train you on tone of voice and use of hand gestures if your problem is related to the previous point

Cons against taking your Goldendoodle to obedience training classes include:

- Classes are usually run once a week; you have to fill in for the other six days of the week
- Different training methods work well for some dogs and not others
- If the majority of the dogs at the training sessions are from more aggressive breeds, the training methods will most likely not be suited to your Goldendoodle
- Cost; obedience training is not a one-day affair, it is an ongoing process, and many training courses are set over a period of four to

six months and more

The choice of professional obedience training or home training your Goldendoodle is completely up to you. You must bear in mind though that professional obedience training classes are not a shortcut that will leave you with a perfectly trained Goldendoodle without you having to put in any effort.

When a dog undergoes obedience training, it has to get to know and understand its trainer and its handler. At professional obedience training classes, you are the handler. For the rest of the week, you have to be both trainer and handler, following the steps that you and your Goldendoodle are taught in the training sessions.

Goldendoodles are classed as working dogs because of their Golden Retriever / Poodle lineage. Working dogs need to be kept busy and stimulated mentally as well as exercised regularly.

To prevent boredom that can lead to destructive or obsessive behaviour, training is vital.

If your Goldendoodle is your household pet and part of your family, then self-training within the home will not be a problem. The early sit, stay, etc. commands are very easy to teach a dog as intelligent as a Goldendoodle. From there you can train your Goldendoodle to play games, how to walk on a lead and how to perform some household tasks.

If your Goldendoodle is going to partake in competitive dog sports, accompany you on hunting trips to retrieve birds and small mammals or going to partake in dog shows, then a professional dog trainer is recommended. It is best to find a trainer who is experienced in training non-aggressive working dogs because they will understand the sensitive nature of Goldendoodles.

3. Obedience Training at Home

As this book is for people wanting to know more about keeping a Goldendoodle as a household pet, the focus will be on training your Goldendoodle to keep busy within the home environment.

Specialist training for dog sports competitions, hunting and retrieving and dog-shows are excluded.

a) Basic Obedience Training

Basic obedience training covers teaching your Goldendoodle commands like sit, stay, lie down, fetch, drop, down, etc. Goldendoodles are not only very intelligent, but they are also eager to please. With time, patience and dedication you will be able to train your Goldendddoodle quite easily. If your Goldendoodle is doted on, spoken to regularly and is part of the household, training will be even easier.

You have to train your Goldendoodle everyday. Training it once a week or once a month is pointless!

Before you begin training your Goldendoodle, it is vital that you decide on which words you are going to use for each command. The word itself is not important, but using the word exclusively for that specific command is. If you are going to include hand gestures, then the same rule must apply. The consistent use of the same word and hand gesture for a specific command is vital.

If obedience training is going to be a family affair involving everyone in the household, then all must use the same words and hand gestures for a specific command. It would be best to make a list for everyone to refer to, to avoid confusing your Goldendoodle.

You must alšo decide if you are going to reward your dog with a treat for doing well, or whether you will use praise alone. For basic obedience training praise alone should be more than enough for a Goldendoodle that is eager to please.

Start off slowly using easy commands like 'sit' and 'stay' for about 15 minutes a few times a day. If you start training at around 6months, your Goldendoodle may still have a reasonably short span of attention. Increase the length and complexity of training sessions as it grows older.

Always make sure that you have your Goldendoodle's full attention before giving a command and that you have eye contact. Commands must be given in a sharp, firm but kindly manner using only the command word/s. Examples of basic commands and hand gestures include:

Sit –your arm extended towards your Goldendoodle, palm open and facing downwards say "sit" while bringing your palm down towards the floor or ground at the same time. Give it a few seconds and if there is no response try again. Keep trying until your Goldendoodle sits. Even if it only sat for a few seconds give it lots of praise in a more relaxed and happy voice tone.

If you have just started obedience training and you can see that your Goldendoodle does not understand, kneel beside it and say "sit" in your training voice while gently putting pressure on its hindquarters with your hand on its back. It should go into a sitting position. Once it does, give it praise. Repeat the command while gently putting it into a sitting position and giving praise a few more times. Once it sits without any pressure applied, it has understood.

Return to standing in front of your Goldendoodle and repeat the verbal and hand sit command simultaneously. Keep trying until it sits and then praise it.

Stay- 'stay' is usually the next step after 'sit' because it is a continuation of the same command. As your Goldendoodle is sitting in front of you, tilt your writs upwards so that your flat palm is facing it and at the same time say "stay" in your training voice. If it gets up without staying sitting, get it's attention again, repeat the "sit" command and hand gesture and follow that immediately with the "stay" command and hand gesture.

If your Goldendoodle sits and stays for only a few seconds, give it lots of praise and repeat the routine.

Lie down - 'lie down' is a further continuation of the 'sit' 'stay' commands. You want your Goldendoodle to go from a sitting position to extending its front paws and lying flat on its stomach with its head up.

Once your Goldendoodle has learned to 'stay' you can introduce the next training step. Drop your hand so that it is level with your arm, palm down and bend your elbow inward towards your chest. Drop your arm slightly while saying "lie down" in your training voice.

Again, if it seems that your Goldendoodle does not understand, keep saying "stay" in your training voice and approach it slowly. Gently pull both front legs forward and place them straight in front of it so that it is lying flat on its stomach, head up and repeat the words "lie down" in your training voice. Give it lots of praise.

Once you think it understands, return to standing in front of your

Goldendoodle. Start the routine from the beginning with "sit", "stay" and "lie down" one after another with the relevant hand gestures. Try to keep the hand gestures flowing as you give the three commands. Give your Goldendoodle lots of praise once it has mastered those three commands.

As you progress you can follow 'lie down' with the 'stay' command and gesture, again keeping your commands and hand gestures flowing. Turn your back on your Goldendoodle when it is lying down and repeat the word "stay" in your training voice. Turn around after a few seconds, and hopefully, your Goldendoodle is still lying on its stomach watching you.

If it is, you and your Goldendoodle are making great progress. The more commands a dog can master over time the easier it becomes for it to master new commands because its mind has opened to being trained.

Fetch and Drop- fetch is used in play or in getting your
Goldendoodle to do household chores (yes, household chores!) Remember Goldendoodles make wonderful service dogs.

'Fetch' can initially be used in games until your Goldendoodle understands it very well together with the next command 'drop'. It's really simple, you throw something, and at the same time, you say "fetch" in your training voice. Instinctively your Goldendoodle will chase after what you have thrown, find it and run back to you with the item in its mouth.

It can be tricky at first, and this is where early training is needed. Most dogs will hold on to what they have in their mouth, so you must teach your Goldendoodle to 'drop' the item.

Once it is standing in front of you, extend your hand towards your Goldendoodle, palm open, cupped and facing upwards with your arm lowered towards its mouth. In your training voice say "drop". In the beginning, it may run off for a short distance and then come back to you, but keep using the hand gesture and command and it will eventually drop the item. Give it plenty of praise and repeat the commands and hand gestures until it drops the item immediately that it has retrieved it.

Don't pull on the item when you are teaching your Goldendoodle the "drop" command. The training session will immediately be transformed into a play session in your Goldendoodle's mind. Most dogs love playing tug of war. Tug of war is for play not for training! Keep training sessions focused and flowing without interruption.

72

Introduce household chores once your Goldendoodle has become accustomed to training. Service breeds are capable of doing a broad range of tasks. For a household pet 'fetch' and 'drop' would be an excellent starting point.

If your Goldendoodle has indoor toys that are packed away in a toy box, you can teach it to pick up its toys. It does take a while, but Goldendoodles can be trained to do it. You would have to introduce more commands and hand gestures, and you would have to imprint the word "toys" and "toy-box" into your Goldendoodles' brain. Imprinting the two words creates a mental association between "toys" and "toy-box".

Something like "fetch your toys" while pointing at the toy-box would be a good start. If you can see that your Goldendoodle does not understand, pick up some of its scattered toys and drop them into the toy-box while repeating the command "fetch your toys" in your training voice. If it picks up a toy and takes it to its toy-box say "drop" again, pointing at the toy-box.

It might take a while, but if you repeatedly follow this routine, you can train your Goldendoodle to pack its toys aways. Likewise, you can train it to bring toys from its toy-box using the "fetch" command and the words "toys" and "toy-box" together with pointing gestures.

This can advance to training your Goldendoodle to fetch your vehicle keys if you are going for a ride, or it can bring it's lead if you are taking it for a walk. You can even train your Goldendoodle to fetch and bring laundry on washdays, as long as you have imprinted the words for the items you want to fetched into its brain.

Training your Goldendoodle to help with household chores will make it feel part of the family. Goldendoodles thrive on human company, are eager to please, are working dogs and excel with 'fetch' and 'drop' tasks. Your Goldendoodle needs the mental stimulation working tasks give, and it will love the praise you give for a job well done.

Down - is a training command that you must use if your Goldendoodle is jumping on your furniture and you don't want it to, or if it is jumping up on anything where you don't want it to be. In your training voice say "down" while simultaneously pointing at the floor. If it ignores you after a few commands, gently lift it from where it is and place it on the floor, repeating the word "down". If its bed is close by, lift it from the furniture and put it in its bed with the command and hand gesture for "stay".

b) *Jumping Up Against People*

It is very common for puppies to jump up against people and when they are very small, it is cute. As they grow older, jumping up is not cute anymore and can frighten and hurt children and even adults in the case of large dogs. Particularly large and medium sized Goldendoodles could unintentionally push a child off its feet. Even an adult could be unexpectedly bowled over by a large dog! If anyone gets hurt, the dog gets the blame; Goldendoodles are loving and sensitive dogs. It's not the Goldendoodle that needs reprimanding; the owner must be reprimanded for failing to train it properly.

Jumping up is a habit that you must stop very early in your Goldendoodle's life. Training it not to jump up works well, but it must be done very gently because you will start the training when it is still a small puppy.

When your Goldendoodle puppy jumps up against you, gently push it over onto its back with a word that you choose as a training command like "no" for example. If it rolls over and jumps up again, repeat the process of gently pushing it over onto its back while repeating your command in your training command voice. If after gently pushing it over it does not jump up again, praise it. Young puppies may take some time to break this habit, but it is a habit that you must break.

As your puppy grows bigger, you can gently lift your knee and flip it over onto it's back while using your training command. Praise it every time that it does not jump up again after being flipped over. It is vital that you repeat this training routine whenever your puppy jumps up against you or someone else. If you allow it sometimes and stop it at other times it could be a very annoying habit that becomes hard to break. Remember always be gentle when flipping the puppy over. It must not feel pain.

c) *Lead Training*

Training your Goldendoodle to walk on a lead from a very young age is important. The younger it is when it learns to walk on a lead, the easier it is for both of you. There are very few places worldwide where you can walk a dog off a lead. Most countries have designated beach or park areas where dogs can run free, but for most areas dogs must be controlled by a collar or harness and lead.

Start off by allowing your Goldendoodle puppy to become accustomed to wearing a collar. Very young puppies can't be taken for walks because their muscles are not well developed and they lack the stamina, but letting them wear a collar from the start cannot harm.

Because puppies grow very fast it is vital to remember to check the collar regularly to ensure that it is not becoming too tight. You should be able to comfortably fit two fingers between the collar and the puppy's neck.

If you have a small sized Goldendoodle you might prefer a harness to a collar, although using a harness on a Goldendoodle would be based on your preference and not necessity. In that case, you would have to buy a harness that can be made bigger and at its smallest size fit it onto your puppy to wear around the house for a few weeks to become accustomed to it. Harnesses must be removed after an hour or so; do not keep it on permanently.

At around 16 weeks of age, you can start training your Goldendoodle to walk with a collar or harness and lead around the house. Clip the lead onto the collar or harness and let it go so that the puppy can run around dragging the lead to become accustomed to the feel of it.

Call your puppy to you using a training command of your choice. "Walk time", "let's go" whatever suits you, but keep it constant. Gently pick up the lead when your puppy approaches you and keeping it slack, walk slowly with your little Goldendoodle around your house or yard. Don't give any command or pull on the lead at this stage; let the puppy lead you. Chat to your puppy as you walk and try to keep the lead slack all the time. Repeat the routine for a few days until your puppy is quite comfortable and does not feel fearful or threatened.

Many dogs will react with fear to something like a lead, a long piece of rope, an electric cord, hosepipe or similar. It is believed to be an instructive reaction to a fear of snakes and the danger snakes pose. Showing your puppy the lead and similar items and letting it sniff at them will break that instinctive fear.

As you keep walking around your house or yard, gently start tightening your hold on the lead, bringing your puppy closer to you and leading the walk rather than following your puppy. There may be resistance, and your puppy could start pulling on the lead wanting to walk in another direction. As soon as that happens, stop walking and stand still without saying a word or making eye contact. Wait for your puppy to return to you and then continue walking, praising your puppy. Repeat this routine at any time that your puppy pulls at the lead to go in another direction.

Large and Medium Goldendoodles grow into strong dogs, so teaching your puppy to walk at your side on a slack lead is very important.

When you and your Goldendoodle puppy are ready, you can take the plunge and venture into the street for your first public walk together. There is no preparing for how it will go because you have no idea what you and your Goldendoodle will encounter on its first time out.

Goldendoodles do not have a natural herding instinct, so its unlikely that your puppy will chase after other dogs, cats, birds, cars, etc. They are also not an aggressive breed, so it's also highly unlikely that your puppy will challenge any other dogs. If your puppy has been well socialised, it should not bark at other dogs or people either.

Allow your puppy to sniff at things that draw its attention and remember to carry a poop-bag with you just in case. In many cities dog owners are fined if they do not pick up their dog's poop on pavements and in other public places.

Your Goldendoodles first public walk could be quite overwhelming for it, and it may tire quite easily, so keep your route short. If your puppy does become very tired it might try to lie down. In that case it is best to pick it up and carry it home.

Very important to remember is that if it is either very hot or very cold, walking on tar or stone surfaces can badly burn or numb your puppies paw pads. Not only when it is a puppy, but always. If it is very hot or very cold, opt for taking your Goldendoodle to a park where it can walk on the grass.

d) Separation Anxiety Prevention

Because Goldendoodles are inclined to separation anxiety, it is best that you address the issue when it is still a small puppy. Put your Goldendoodle puppy outside in a safe, secure and shaded place, or in a playpen indoors on its own with lots of dog chews and toys. Turn your back on it and walk away casually and close the door behind you without any fanfare. Ignore it if it cries and whines. Because puppies have a short attention span, its mind will easily be diverted to its dog chews and toys. It might even fall asleep.

Leave it for a while to learn to keep itself busy. When you come to let it indoors or take it from its playpen, do so without saying anything or making any fuss. Continue including it in your routines as normal from thereon. Repeat this routine daily.

4. Reading Body Language

Dogs read humans through eye contact, the tone of the human's voice and by reading human body language. Dogs give humans many communication cues but because so many people believe dogs are stupid (dumb-dog!), their ignorance makes them overlook what the dog is telling them. All dog-lovers will tell you that dogs communicate with humans. People who work with dogs daily in law enforcement or military canine units, in search and rescue units and who work with service dogs often say that they know what their dogs are communicating to them and they feel safer when their dog is by their side than when any human is by their side.

Your Goldendoodle instinctively knows how to read you and understands what you communicate to it. It instinctively reads your moods as well, and many dogs will comfort their owners if they begin to cry, are ill or are depressed. With a little effort, you too can learn to understand what your Goldendoodle is telling you.

No one can deny the expression of joy and happiness on a dogs face when its owner comes home. If you can identify that, there is so much more you can learn about communication between dogs and humans.

Communication does not require words. Pay attention to your Goldendoodle's facial expressions and body language, and the two of you will be able to communicate quite easily. Because your dog offers no spoken word, the code of communication that develops between a person and a dog that have a close bond can be unique and other people might overlook it.

Seeing as Goldendoodles need to be part of the family and included in the household, your Goldendoodle will spend a lot of time with you. Speak openly to it from the day you bring it home. When it gets older and follows you around wherever you go, tell it what you are busy doing; allow it to smell things and look closely at things that you are handling. Dogs do learn enough vocabulary to understand commands and basic conversations.

A dog can also 'tell the time' if you share your scheduled routine with it. Your Goldendoodle will come and call you around say 6:00 pm if you always start preparing dinner at 6:00 pm. Once you take notice, it will walk straight to the kitchen. If you leave for work every day at around 7:30 am it will start walking towards the door at that time to see you off.

a) Common Communication Signals

Here are some of the more common communication signals that your Goldendoodle will give you:

- **Curiosity** - eyes wide open, head tilting from one side to another; it may edge closer to get a sniff of what's going on "Show me too please!"

- **Happy** - doggy-smile from ear-to-ear; tail wagging wildly "We're going for a walk!" or "Hello – I'm happy you're home!"

- **Shame** - mostly lying flat on its stomach with its head on its forelegs, but could be sitting with head hanging low, giving upward glances "I'm sorry I shredded the toilet paper again!" or "I'm sorry I chewed your shoe!"

- **Pleading -** head tilted to one side, eyes staring into yours sadly. The expression is beseeching to play on your emotions and make you feel guilty "But why not?" Pleading, usually for a treat or to go for a walk or something similar; it works well and you will mostly cave in.

- **Stretching back and forth** - when waking up or after lazing about "I'm comfortable and happy!"

- **Pawing or pushing** - a call for attention. Signs of anxiety could indicate pain or danger. Mostly it is "You're ignoring me. I want your love and attention."

- **Front legs flat down, hindquarters up -** a happy and playful signal "I want to play!"

- **Belly-up -** a trusting pose and a call for attention "Please give me a belly rub!"

78

- **Licking you** - a gesture of love and affection "I love you!"

- **Rolling on your dirty laundry** - a huge compliment! Particularly unwashed items that are worn close to your body like socks, stockings and underwear that have most of your scent on them. "I love you so much I want to smell like you!"

There are also communication signals that your Goldendoodle can give you when you are out walking together or exercising and playing in a park. Goldendoodles are not known to be aggressive, but it could encounter aggression from other dogs that could cause it to react in different ways. These include:

- **Body rigid, legs spread** - alert and suspicious. Focused on something that does not make it feel comfortable "What's this?" or "What's going on?"

- **Cowering** - cowering is an indication of fear. Look around to see what is causing the fear, bearing in mind that a dog's sense of hearing and smell is much better than yours "I'm afraid!"

- **Cowering while barking** - cowering while barking is also an indication of fear, but your dog is willing to defend itself "I'm afraid, but I'll fight back."

- **Constantly licking its nose** – constantly licking its nose (licking every few seconds) is a sign of stress "I don't like this situation!"

Many puppies become frightened by big birds like geese, noisy vehicles like motorbikes and a myriad of sights and sounds that they have never seen or heard before. As they grow older and go on regular walks and outings, they lose this fear.

It is important that you always investigate the cause of your Goldendoodles fear and anxiety because it could potentially be being threatened by another dog and you don't want your Goldendoodle to become involved in a dogfight!

b) How to Handle a Dog Fight

Although Goldendoodles are not an aggressive breed, many other dog breeds are innately aggressive, and many dog owners are reckless.

Aggressive dogs are dangerous to other dogs, cats and people. Owners of aggressive dogs should keep them on a lead and harness, not a collar. A harness fits across the dog's chest and back, giving the owner far more control over the dog. A harness is very unlikely to snap, whereas a collar can snap under extreme pressure.

Although your Goldendoodle could encounter an aggressive dog when walking along a pavement, aggressive encounters are more likely to happen in open areas like parks and beaches. It is advisable to always take a walking stick along with you when taking your Goldendoodle to open areas in case you need to ward off another dog.

As you are walking and let your Goldendoodle run loose, make sure that you do not lose sight of it and that you are constantly watching its body language. If it is playing with other dogs, keep an eye on their body language as well. It is easier to stop a dogfight before it happens than it is to break up a dogfight.

Small dogs are particularly vulnerable in spontaneous dogfights if attacked by a bigger dog. A big dog can kill a small dog in a matter of seconds. If you own a small sized Goldendoodle, consider very carefully if you want to let in run loose in a public space where there are lots of other bigger dogs.

If a dogfight breaks out, other aggressive dogs can join the fight, and more passive dogs will run away. Signs of aggression to look for in other dogs include:

- A dog that constantly mounts one or some other dogs (a sign of bullying and testing its strength)
- A dog that constantly shadows one or some other dogs (intimidation)
- A dog that pins one or some other dogs down in play and holds them down while keeping it's body rigid (bullying and show of strength)
- A dog that harasses one or some dogs by running around them and snapping at them, even if they are trying to get away (bullying)
- A dog that stares at another dog with a fixed gaze while keeping its body rigid (aggressive challenge)
- A dog or dogs that are snarling, lips raised and teeth bared (blatant aggressive challenge)

- A dog or dogs that have a rigid body stance with hackles up at the shoulders (blatant aggressive challenge)

If you observe any of these signs of aggression in another dog that is close to your Goldendoodle, call it away immediately. If it does not come to you, go and fetch it before there are any aggressive interactions even if the aggression is not geared towards your Goldendoodle.

If another dog does attack your Goldendoodle, remember that fighting dogs are focused only on each other. Your aim must be to distract one or both of the fighting dogs for long enough to separate them and keep them separated.

Actions you can take if another dog attcks your Goldendoodle:

- Keep away from the centre of the fight whether your Goldendoodle is fighting back or not (putting your hands between the heads of fighting dogs to try and separate them will result in one, or both of them biting you)
- Don't grab your Goldendoodle by its collar either because your Goldendoodle could mistake it for another attack and bite you when it turns around (remember both dogs are in a high state of emotional arousal and possibly panic)
- Keep behind them and try to separate them by distraction
- If there is a garbage can, large cooler box or any other item that will make a loud noise if banged on - bang on it repeatedly
- If there is anything rigid nearby like a plank or piece of board try putting that between their muzzles
- If there is a vehicle close by ask the owner to hoot repeatedly or drive towards them if possible to distract them
- If there is access to water close by pour it over their faces; a hose is even better, spray them
- Never pull either dog by the tail because you can break sensitive nerves in the tail that control bladder and bowel movements
- Instead, lift your Goldendoodles hind legs from the ground and pull it backwards; this will work well if someone can do the same with the other dog
- If the other dog has your Goldendoodle down on its back, try kicking the other dog away but only if you are wearing shoes with thick soles and long pants

Dogfights are very traumatic to witness, and because Goldendoodles are not an aggressive breed, your Goldendoodle will most likely be highly traumatised. Once the dogs are separated, get your Goldendoodle away from the scene and out of sight of the other dog as quickly as possible.

If you can see that your Goldendoodle is bleeding take it to the nearest vet without delay! Dog bites can be very deep and can cause severe (and even fatal) bleeding. Dog bites can also become septic very easily because of bacteria in the mouth of all dogs. Your Goldendoodle will probably be in shock, and a sedative, as well as an anti-inflamatory injection will also help. Depending on its injuries, the vet will clean it up, stitch it and send it home with pain and anti-inflammatory tablets as well as antibiotics. If the injuries are serious the vet might admit your Goldendoodle as an inpatient for more intensive treatment. Sometimes dogs that have been attacked can suffer from severe shock and trauma and many vets would prefer to keep them at their practice for at least a few hours to ensure that they calm down without side-effects.

Chapter 10. Healthy Diet

A diet of high-quality pellets, tinned meat and biscuits will give your Goldendoodle a balanced diet that is more than enough to keep it healthy. Make sure that you follow the portion size provided on the packaging that suits your Goldendoodle's weight to avoid under or overfeeding.

Try to keep mealtimes routine by feeding your Goldendoodle at the same time each day. Adult dogs should be fed twice a day and a small treat between meals won't do any harm as long as the treat portions are kept small and limited to only once or twice a day.

1) Foods that are Unhealthy

As tempting as it may be, do not feed your Goldendoodle food from your plate or left-over's after meals. There are certain foods that are not healthy for dogs. Unnatural flavouring, salt, sugar and spices do not compliment a dog's digestive system and can cause vomiting or worse.

It's worth a mention that dogs are omnivores and need to eat meat (animal protein). Dogs cannot survive on plant proteins because their digestive systems differ from that of a human being. Feeding your dog only plant proteins like soya mince, etc. will lead to emaciation, starvation and death. Feeding your dog only carbohydrates like bread, rice or porridge with a broth poured over will have the same result.

Human foods that you should not feed your Goldendoodle include:

- Alcohol - never! Not only is it bad for dogs, but common logic also says it's cruel to give any animal a mind-altering substance
- Artificial sweeteners - so no 'sugar free' anything, including peanut butter
- Avocado
- Candy and chocolate
- Chicken bones
- Citrus fruits
- Coffee
- Cooked animal bones*
- Dairy products
- Fast food - of any kind! They are all laced with salt, spices and sugar

- Garlic
- Grapes and raisins
- Mushrooms
- Nuts - almonds, macadamia and walnuts
- Onions
- Potato - raw
- Salt
- Soft drinks
- Spices
- Sugar
- Tea

*Cooked or roasted animal bones become brittle and can splinter when gnawed. These splinters can cut your Goldendoodles mouth and digestive tract. Hollow rounds of marrow bone can become lodged between your Goldendoodle's teeth and require surgical removal.

These are only some of the foods that you should not feed your Goldendoodle. Although some of these foods might not cause serious harm if eaten in small amounts, others can make your dog very ill. Some foods that will do no harm in small amounts could start to do harm if small amounts are fed regularly to your Goldendoodle.

Constantly changing your Goldendoodle's diet can also cause digestive problems and stomach upsets. Unlike humans, dogs are quite content to eat the same food every day.

2) Foods that are Healthy

Human foods that you can feed your dog include:

- Apples
- Bananas
- Berries
- Carrots
- Cucumber
- Cherries - remove pit
- Eggs
- Honey
- Mango - remove the pit
- Oatmeal

- Peaches - remove the pit
- Peanut butter - preferably organic, salt and sugar-free (bland)
- Pasta - boiled without salt
- Potato - boiled/baked without salt
- Rice - boiled without salt
- Sweet potato - boiled/baked without salt
- Zucchini

When feeding your Goldendoodle fruit, remove all pits and tough peels that can be potential choking hazards. Large Goldendoodles can have a whole or big piece of carrot, cucumber or zucchini to chew. Small Goldendoodles should only have whole baby carrots, baby cucumber or baby zucchini, or portions of these vegetables cut into sticks. Never overfeed on fruit and raw vegetables. Allow only small amounts every day because if eaten in excess they can lead to stomach cramps and diarrhoea.

3) Healthy Homemade Treats

In between meal treats should be small and healthy. You might not have the time to prepare special homemade treats for your Goldendoodle, but some are really quick and easy to make. Here are a few ideas for quick and easy homemade treats:

a) Sweet Potato Treats

Ingredients

Sweet potatoes or yams (golden sweet potatoes)

Method

- Pre-heat oven to 250° Fahrenheit (120° Celsius / Gas Mark 1 or 2)
- Line a baking tray with parchment paper
- Wash a large sweet potato and dry well
- Cut into strips or rounds of 1 ¼ Centimetres (½ Inch)
- Spread slices or strips evenly on baking tray
- Bake in preheated oven for 3 hours
- Cool on a wire rack

Sweet potatoes are packed with vitamins and minerals and these sweet potato treats take no time to prepare. The preparation time is no more than

85

10 minutes and the rest of the time is spent in slow baking them into a healthy chewy treat that your Goldendoodle will love!

These sweet potato treats will keep well in a fridge in a covered container for about five days.

b) *Apple Carrot Treats*

Ingredients:

1 Cup whole wheat or brown rice flour
1 Cup freshly grated carrot
1 Egg
½ Cup unsweetened apple puree

Method

- Preheat oven to 350° Fahrenheit (177° Celsius / Gas Mark 4)
- Line a baking tray with parchment paper
- Mix all ingredients to form a dough
- Roll dough into small, medium or large balls (to suit the size of your Goldendoodle)
- Flatten each ball with your hand to form a round
- Bake in preheated oven until golden brown
- Cool on a wire rack

Dogs love apples and carrots, and these treats make a tasty alternative to dog biscuits. If you want a chewy texture, keep them thicker. For a more crunchy texture, flatten them more to allow them to dry out while baking. Prepare them in a size that is easy for your Goldendoodle to chew.

These apple and carrot treats will keep well in a covered container, kept in a cool, dry place for about five days.

c) *Banana, Peanut Butter & Honey Treat*

Ingredients

1 Egg
½ Cup mashed banana
1 Tablespoon honey
4 Tablespoons peanut butter (preferably organic salt and sugar-free)

1 Cup whole wheat flour

Method

- Preheat oven to 300° Fahrenheit (150° Celsius / Gas Mark 2)
- Line a baking tray with parchment paper
- Thoroughly combine the egg, banana, honey and peanut butter in a mixing bowl
- Add the whole wheat flour and mix in well to form a dough
- Turn dough out onto a floured surface
- Roll dough out to a thickness of about 4 Millimetres or ¼ Inch
- Cut into shapes using a cookie cutter or small drinking glass
- Bake in preheated oven for about 30 minutes depending on size
- Cool on a wire rack

Peanut butter is an absolute winner with all dogs. A tasty and healthy treat that you can give to your Goldendoodle inbetween meals!

These apple and carrot treats will keep well in a covered container, kept in a cool dry place for about a week.

d) Meaty Jerky Treat

Ingredients

Any fresh meat fillets, including fish, poultry, beef, lamb, mutton or game.

You will also need a raised wire cooling rack or oven-proof trivet to allow the heat in the oven to distribute evenly around the meat.

Method

- Preheat oven to 200° Fahrenheit (100° Celsius / Gas Mark 1)
- Line a baking tray with tin foil
- Trim off any excess fat from meat
- Slice meat into long, thin slivers cutting with the grain (keep thickness and length the same to allow for even dehydration)
- Place wire cooling rack or trivet inside tin foil lined baking tray
- Place meat strips evenly on wire rack or trivet
- Bake for approximately 2 to 3 hours, turning every 30 minutes or until meat is thoroughly dehydrated (this will depend on the type of meat that you used)

- Allow to cool completely

No words required! Meat jerky will be a winner with your Goldendoodle. You can use any cut of meat, including liver. Tuna and salmon also make great jerky (remember to remove all bones).
Whatever meat you decide to use, you will find that you can slice slivers more easily using a sharp knife if the meat is half-frozen.

Meat jerky must be stored in your fridge or freezer because it is preservative and salt-free. The jerky must not be exposed to water (it will rehydrate), so it is best kept in your fridge in a brown paper bag. It will keep for up to 3 weeks in your fridge. If you opt for freezing, also put the jerky in a brown paper bag.

Chapter 11. Identifying the Cause of Bad Behaviour

There are four prime catalysts of destructive behaviour in dogs:

- Poor training
- Boredom
- Emotional/ Mental Health Problems
- Disease

All dogs have to be trained to behave well and in a manner that suits their household and surroundings.

If you want to own a dog, you have to invest time in obedience training. A dog is like a small child; if it is not taught good behaviour, manners and hygiene it won't learn them on its own.

Many people will say that they tried to train their dog, but it didn't work. If you can't train your dog, there are many professional dog trainers who will give you advice and train your dog properly.

There is no excuse for having a dog that has not been given obedience training!

Boredom is common in dogs that are locked out and ignored, getting very little attention other than a bowl of food. Dogs need space, company (human or canine), dog chews and toys to play with and keep them busy.

Goldendoodles are intelligent working and service dogs. They must be included in the family and household! They want to be part of the conversation; they need regular exercise and they need mental stimulation.

They also need lots of dog-chews and toys to keep them occupied.

A clear line must be drawn between what a dog owner calls destructive behaviour based on their expectations of how a dog 'should' behave, and genuine destructive behaviour.

All healthy dogs bark, dig in the garden (or in indoor pot plants), steal opportunistically (anything from a sock to food), get spurts of energy and runs around the garden at great speed, or up and down your passage, roll on the grass and then walk into your house, etc. This is not 'bad' or 'destructive' behaviour; it is dog behaviour! In addition, certain breeds have innate traits to chase, burrow, hunt and guard. If you buy a dog without studying the breed characteristics you can end up with a dog that does not suit your household.

Movies can also influence peoples' choice of dog as a household pet. In the movie, the breed of dog plays a certain role that is projected onto the public's mind. People go and buy dogs of this breed expecting them to behave like the dog in the movie, and when it doesn't they brand it as a 'bad' dog, and it ends up in a rescue shelter. Irresponsible pet ownership!

A perfect example of this type of 'misidentification' of a dog breeds' characteristics is the movie "101 Dalmatians" depicting cute Dalmatians. After seeing this movie, countless parents worldwide ran out to buy their children a Dalmatian puppy.

Movies sell entertainment and fantasy! Real Dalmatian puppies grow into active, strong medium-sized guard dogs. Their lineage is from working dogs, and there is a belief that they were used at one time as war-dogs, fighting in the thick of hand-to-hand battle. They need physical and mental stimulation and are not suited to small yards or apartment living. Well-intentioned, but ignorant Dalmatian owners who had bought the puppies for their children and did not know how to handle the breed branded them as 'bad' or 'destructive' and rescue shelters worldwide were flooded with Dalmatians.

The Dalmatian breed suffered greatly as a result of the movie "101 Dalmatians". A dog is part of the real-world and must be understood to be a real-world sentient being. It is not an object of fashion or fantasy!

1. Destructive Behaviour

Genuine destructive behaviour is an extension of normal destructive behaviour and can include the excessive destruction of your garden, tipping your garbage bin over, jumping fences and chewing at wooden doors. This behaviour usually occurs when the owners are not home and are an extension of a dog's normal exploratory instinct (curiosity).

If your Goldendoodle is guilty of any (or all and more) of the above behaviours, more in-depth obedience training and more regular exercise can solve the problem. Also, give your Goldendoodle many more dog chews and toys to keep it busy and offer it variety.

Unfortunately, if you want to keep a dog, you have to accept that your garden will have to put up with some digging. Fence jumping is a serious issue, so you will have to either increase the height of your fence or confine your Goldendoodle to an area of the yard where it is unable to escape when you are not home.

If you can't remedy the situation on your own, call in the services of a professional dog behaviourist to assist.

2. Excessive Barking

All dogs bark and some breeds bark more than others. Normal barking includes protecting their territory, greeting and fear. If your Goldendoodle barks excessively only when you are not home it is most likely boredom, loneliness, separation anxiety (covered in the next sub-chapter) or a medical condition.

All dogs are social animals and thrive on canine or human company. If they are left alone for long periods of time, they can become lonely and start barking, or calling. If you are away for some hours daily, it is best that you get your Goldendoodle a canine companion to play and communicate with while you are away.

If your Goldendoodle barks excessively when you are at home it could be boredom or seeking attention. If it is boredom, you are not keeping it busy enough. Longer walks, more play and more mental stimulation with dog chews and toys can solve the problem.

If it is seeking attention, you need to do some investigation to find out why. Is your Goldendoodle included in household activities, do you and your family play games with it and take it for walks? Many people over-play a puppy, and when the dog gets older, they tend to exclude it from activities because it is much bigger and may get in their way. If that is the case, your family needs a re-think. Goldendoodles must be included in the family for their wellbeing. Are your 'no dogs on the furniture', 'no dirty paws on the clean carpet' type rules causing this loving and sensitive dog to be excluded?

As with a garden, if you want to own any type of dog you have to be willing to accept that dogs, like children, leave mud on floors, prints on carpets and turn the room over making a mess sometimes. Anything that can be fixed with a broom or some soap and water is not a calamity.

Carpets and furniture get old and get replaced - love endears long after the soul has moved on.

3. Separation Anxiety

Goldendoodles are inclined to separation anxiety, so its best addressed in early obedience training.

If not addressed early on and separation anxiety sets in, your Goldendoodle can start acting out even before you leave home. Reading cues that you are going to leave the house can trigger separation anxiety. If your Goldendoodle is kept outdoors while you are away from home, you might have to chase it around the house to get it out. It could hide away from you under beds or behind furniture, and you might have to physically carry your Goldendoodle to the door to put it out.

This routine is stressful for both of you! As you walk or drive away you can hear your Goldendoodle howling and barking - it can have a very emotional effect on you.

While you are away your Goldendoodle can act out on its anxiety by howling, whining, barking and digging frantically to get out of the house or out of the yard. The attempts to escape can be frantic and result in your Goldendoodle injuring itself. It can also run around frantically, tipping over anything that's in its way.

When you return home, you can find your Goldendoodle to be overactive, jumping up on you and shadowing you wherever you go. It can take quite a while before it calms down.

Separation anxiety must be addressed and treated for your Goldendoodle's sake, your sake and your neighbour's sake because a dog barking and howling endlessly can become more than an irritation.

If your Goldendoodle was not trained to cope with your absences and separation anxiety sets in when it is older, deal with it as soon as you become aware of it.

When going out, leave without any greetings and fanfare. It is the goodbye and fanfare that goes with it that often triggers separation anxiety. Calmly walk out without looking back. When you arrive back home later, open the door, and if your Goldendoodle has been outside let it in without saying a word, patting it or making eye contact. Ignore your Goldendoodle until it calms down. Once it has calmed down, greet it and pat it without any overt excitement. If it gets over excited again, ignore it again until it is calm. Repeat the routine, and it could begin to reverse separation anxiety.

You can also try making changes to your leaving routine like placing items that your Goldendoodle associates with you leaving, like your car keys or handbag, close to the door long before you leave so that it does not see the items. Calmly walk to the door and lead your Goldendoodle out without a word, or close the door behind you without a word. Avoid eye contact as well. Whether your Goldendoodle stays inside or outside while you are away, make sure that it has plenty of dog chews and toys to keep it busy during your absence.

If none of the above work call in the services of a professional dog behaviourist to assist.

Dogs that suffer from separation anxiety, even if it is controlled separation anxiety, should not be left at boarding kennels while you are out of town. It is best to get a house-sitter so that your Goldendoodle's daily routine and environment are left undisturbed. Professional house-sitters are best because they will interact with your Goldendoodle. A friend of family might choose to just stop by daily to see that your Goldendoodle is fine and feed it.

4. Repetitive Obsessive Behaviours

Repetitive obsessive behaviours are performed to reduce stress, are time-consuming and interfere with the dog's normal behaviour or routine.

The behaviours vary but can include shadow chasing, circling, excessive licking of its coat resulting in dermatitis, plucking at its coat causing hair loss, constant fly-snapping and fence-running. These behaviours are repeated constantly and take preference over normal human/canine or canine/canine interaction and play.

There are a vast number of causes or triggers of repetitive obsessive behaviours but are mostly as a result of your Goldendoodle being denied adequate space to engage in normal play and exercise, unethical breeding practices and being separated from its mother too soon or as a result of a neurological disorder.

If your Goldendoodle is kept in an area that does not allow it enough space to practice normal dog behaviour such as running, playing digging, etc. then you have to address the situation as a matter of urgency. An example would be a large Goldendoodle being kept in an apartment, not being walked regularly and being left alone for extended periods.

If you have underestimated the size that your Goldendoodle would reach as an adult dog, it is a kinder option to have it adopted through a rescue network than to keep it in your apartment because you have bonded. Many adoptive dog-parents will gladly allow you to visit your Goldendoodle and spend time with it, or update you on how it is doing by sending you pictures regularly.

If your Goldendoodle displays repetitive, obsessive behaviours, it is best to call in the services of a professional dog behaviourist for advice or take your dog to your vet to discuss the symptoms, potential causes and treatment.

5. Hyperactivity

It is important to remember that all puppies and young dogs are very active before you brand your Goldendoodle as 'hyperactive'. A healthy Goldendoodle can be very busy and have a lot of energy that must be expended! Most dogs dumped at rescue shelters because they are 'hyperactive' are not given enough exercise and stimulation by their owners. A dog that does not get enough attention, exercise and stimulation through play will find other means to expend its energy.

Most dogs branded as 'hyperactive' are not hyperactive. They are healthy dogs that need some obedience training, routine, regular exercise and lots of play.

If you think that your Goldendoodle is hyperactive, it is best to best to call in the services of a professional dog behaviourist to teach you how to handle it.

6. Aggression

All dogs will respond with aggression if they feel threated, and even non-aggressive breeds like Goldendoodles can and will bite under pressure.

Overly aggressive behaviour, however, is cause for concern, especially in a Goldendoodle. Because Goldendoodles are a hybrid breed, unless you bought your Goldendoodle from an ethical and reputable breeder it could have aggressive genetic traits from an aggressive breed of dog in its lineage.

Dogs who are innately aggressive will bully and show aggression to other dogs in the home or dogs that they meet while going on walks and outings. They can also display food aggression within the home and try to chase smaller or less aggressive canine companions off their food bowl and eat their food.

Deal with food aggression by always supervising mealtimes and keeping food bowls far apart. Stand between the dogs until all have finished eating. It is best to pick up all empty food bowls immediately and not allow the aggressive dog to walk around licking other empty bowls. Allowing it to lick the other dogs bowls can reinforce the trait of wanting to eat what the other dog or dogs have. By picking up the empty food bowls immediately you are enforcing the rule that each dog has their own bowl and their own food that is not for sharing.

If your Goldendoodle is food aggressive, never spread or throw any treats or food out for the dogs to share. Doing that is almost guaranteed to cause an attack because the food-aggressive Goldendoodle will want it all for itself and if another dog picks up anything it can prompt aggression.

One of the games encouraged to keep Goldendoodles mentally stimulated is to hide treats for it to find. If it is food aggressive, this game is best avoided.

If your Goldendoodle bullies one of your other dogs by constant shadowing, mounting, pinning it down, challenging it if it enters a room or blocking it's way if it wants to leave a room, you need to address this on a daily and constant basis. Every time you see it happening you must intervene in a firm but kind manner.

Find a single word or sequence of words that you use repetitively only to address your Goldendoodle's aggression towards the other dog or dogs. You can use this at feeding time as well if your Goldendoodle begins venturing towards another dog's food bowl while it is still eating. Also, have a specific hand gesture used exclusively for aggression and use it simultaneously with your selected word/s. A good example would be to use the words "back-off" while pointing your index finger, arm extended directly at your Goldendoodle and making direct eye contact. Pointing your index finger with your arm extended directly towards any dog can be very intimidating for the dog and your Goldendoodle will most like retreat quickly. Once it does, give it praise and encourage the other dog to continue with what it wanted to do.

Be aware though that in some of the more aggressive breeds of dogs, and particularly in unneutered males of those breeds, an index finger pointed directly at them with arm extended and direct eye contact can be seen as a challenge and can prompt aggression towards you.

Avoid encouraging any competition between your dogs and treat them all equally. Also avoid rough play or play-fighting with your Goldendoodle when it is a puppy. Rough play, play-fighting and over-playing a puppy can lead to it retaining these behaviors as the adult dog. When it is a small puppy, this type of behaviour can be viewed as cute and cheeky, but in an adult dog, it can be dangerous and concerning. If you did encourage rough-play and play-fighting in your Goldendoodle puppy, you have effectively trained it to become an aggressive adult.

Re-training is required (and is possible) because a house with an aggressive dog is always tense, and everyone in the household shares this tension; human, canine, feline - everyone!

Use the above training method repeatedly every day for any sign of aggressive behaviour. If you are unable to bring the situation under control, it is best to call in the services of a professional dog behaviourist to teach you how to handle it.

Because Goldendoodles are not normally innately aggressive and are more inclined to kindness and affection, if your Goldendoodle suddenly becomes aggressive towards you, other family members or household pets, it could be due to internal pain.

The aggression displayed is out of fear of being pushed, touched or picked-up while it is experiencing internal pain. Even if your Goldendoodle looks healthy and is eating normally, it could still have a painful medical condition. Take it to your vet for a thorough health check as soon as possible.

Remember, dogs do not share the fear that humans attach to disease and a potentially dire diagnosis. That is why they could continue to function normally, despite experiencing pain and discomfort.

Chapter 11. Health and Veterinary Care

1. Vaccinations

Puppies are given either a first and second set of vaccinations, or a first second and third set of vaccinations in the first weeks of their life. Whether they are given a set of two vaccinations or a set of three vaccinations is determined by the veterinary practice, and varies from one country to another. The types of vaccinations are standard though.

All puppies must be given their first vaccinations at between 6 to 8 weeks of age. The next vaccination will be at around 10 weeks of age, and if the vet works on a three vaccination standard, the last vaccination will be three weeks later.

After that all adult dogs must be vaccinated annually around the anniversary of their last vaccinations.

The first puppy vaccination is a mild dose protection against:

- **Bordetella Bronchiseptica** - a highly contagious bacterial infection that causes severe coughing, vomiting, seizure and potentially death; it is the primary cause of what is commonly known as 'kennel cough' .

- **Canine Distemper** - a highly contagious viral infection that attacks the respiratory, gastrointestinal and nervous system of dogs. It causes discharge for the eyes and nose, fever, coughing, diarrhoea, vomiting, involuntary twitching, seizures, paralysis and often death. There is no treatment for Canine Distemper so early vaccination is essential.

- **Canine Parainfluenza** - a highly contagious viral infection that attacks the respiratory system and can lead to tracheobronchitis. It causes coughing, nasal discharge, fever, lethargy and loss of apetite.

The second round of puppy vaccinations are stronger and are commonly referred to as DHPP. If this is to be the final puppy vaccination for the next year, it will be increased to include, Bordetella, Coronavirus, Leptospirosis, Lyme Disease and Rabies. DHPP includes:

- **Distemper**

- **Hepatitis (Adenovirus)** - a highly contagious viral infection that attacks the eyes, liver, lungs, kidney and spleen, causing abdominal pain and swelling, fever, congestion, jaundice and vomiting. It can be fatal, and there is no cure. Early vaccination is essential; it is unrelated to Hepatitis in humans.

- **Parainfluenza**

- **Parvovirus** - a highly contagious viral infection that attacks the gastrointestinal system causing fever, loss of appetite, vomiting and bloody diarrhoea. Young puppies under 4 months of age are particularly susceptible and they can die within 48 hours due to extreme dehydration. Older dogs are also susceptible, and it can be fatal as there is no cure. Early vaccination is essential.

Additional vaccinations that could be included offer protection against:

- **Coronavirus** - a viral infection that attacks the gastrointestinal system and occasionally the respiratory system as well. It causes loss of appetite, nausea, vomiting and diarrhoea. There is no cure and it can be fatal. Early vaccination is essential.

- **Leptospirosis** - a bacterial infection that causes loss of appetite, fever, vomiting, diarrhoea, jaundice, muscle stiffness and pain, kidney failure and liver failure. It can be treated with antibiotics if diagnosed quickly. It is transmittable to humans.

- **Lyme Disease** - also known as Borreliosis, it is an infectious tick-borne disease caused by a bacteria called Spirochete. Initial symptoms include loss of appetite, fever, limping and swollen lymph nodes. Left untreated the disease can affect the heart, kidneys, liver, joints and have serious neurological complications. If diagnosed quickly it can be successfully treated with antibiotics, but relapse can occur.

- **Rabies** - a viral infection that invades the central nervous system causing anxiety, headaches, hallucinations, excessive drooling, paralysis and potentially death. It is most commonly spread through the bite of an infected animal. Without a quick diagnosis, it is almost always fatal. Early vaccination is essential. Rabies is transmittable to humans.

If a third round of vaccinations is given, it is usually a repeat of the DHPP vaccinations. Some vets prefer to include some of the above-mentioned vaccines with the third round of vaccinations rather than with the second.

2. Internal Parasites

Worms are the most common internal parasites found in dogs. Most puppies are born with intestinal Round Worms transmitted from their mother through lactation. Deworming is essential from a very young age. The most common worms found in dogs include:

- **Heart Worm** – are spread by mosquitoes and contamination is preventable with regular prophylactic medication. Larvae lodge in the right side of the heart from where they can spread to other organs causing injury and blockage. There are no early symptoms, but severe infestation causes fatigue, lethargy, loss of appetite, breathing difficulties and ultimately organ failure.

- **Round Worms** - are often transmitted through lactation when larvae pass from mother to pup. Round worm larvae can also be transmitted from mother to pup in-utero from the mother's tissue. They infest the puppies' intestinal tract. If left untreated they can cause emaciation and ultimately death through intestinal blockage

- **Hook Worms** - are often transmitted through lactation on in-utero. They migrate to the small-intestine and latch on the walls to feed off blood. If left untreated they can easily kill small puppies by causing severe anaemia from blood loss. In older dogs, they cause emaciation, lethargy and a compromised immune system that can make the dog susceptible to other illness as a result of anaemia.

- **Tape Worms** - are transmitted to dogs by fleas. They latch themselves to the walls of the digestive tract and feed off the stomach contents. If left untreated they can cause emaciation and starvation. Over-the-counter generic medicines will not kill them: the infestation must be treated by a vet.

- **Whip Worms** - lodge themselves in the first section of the large-intestine and feed off the stomach contents. They can cause emaciation and starvation. They are difficult to detect, and infestations must be treated by a vet.

All worms discussed above except Heart Worm are passed on to adult dogs through feceas of an infected cat or dog. The feceas contain larvae and eggs, and these are ingested by puppies and adult dogs from the ground around the faeces or by ingestion of the faceas.

Puppies are dewormed for the first time at the same time that they are vaccinated for the first time. Some breeders will start de-worming small puppies from 2 weeks of age and every second week after that until they are 12 weeks old because many puppies are born with worms.

After their last round of vaccinations or last puppy de-worming, all puppies and dogs should be de-wormed every three months for the rest of their life.

3. External Parasites

If your Goldendoodle is a household pet that lives indoors, you must take preventative treatment for internal and external parasites. A well cared for dog that is groomed regularly should not have many parasitic infestations. If an infestation is identified and treated immediately, it will clear very rapidly. The most common parasites that your Goldendoodle will encounter include:

- **Fleas** - that will most likely be picked up when going for walks (particularly in parks and in the country-side) or from over-night kennels and grooming parlours. Fleas crawl along a dog's coat onto the skin and suck blood through the skin. They will be immediately visible if you brush your Goldendoodle regularly. Symptoms are constant scratching and inflamed skin. Some dogs have an allergy to flea bites and that can cause dermatitis.

  There are many treatments for flea infestations that include sprays, shampoos and dips. Prevention is the best option and quality sprays that are regularly sprayed into your Goldendoodle's coat and around your house are the best deterrent.

- **Ticks** - are picked up from grassy areas and bushes. They detect their host from body heat and on contact crawl through the coat and burrow into an area of skin to feed off blood. Ticks are clearly visible if you brush your Goldendoodle regularly.

There are topical treatments available that repel ticks and ticks can also be removed with a special device available from pet product retailers. Once a tick is removed and killed, no further treatment is necessary.

Ticks can spread a variety of serious disease that varies from country to country and on the type of tick. If your Goldendoodle displays any sign of illness after you have found a tick on it, take it to your vet immediately and advise the vet that you removed a tick or ticks. Also, show the vet where on your Goldendoodles body each tick was removed.

- **Mosquitoes** - are flying insects that draw blood from its hosts' skin. In some countries, mosquitoes spread Heart Worm. Mosquitoes are prevalent in the warmer months of the year and proliferate around areas where there is stagnant water.

  It is difficult to prevent your Goldendoodle from being bitten by mosquitoes, but some topical treatments that contain the ingredient Imidacloprid for repelling fleas and ticks also do repel mosquitoes.

- **Lice and Mites** - are both tiny parasites that burrow into the flesh and feed off blood. There are many different types of mites in particular.

  If your Goldendoodle is an indoor dog that is a part of your household and family, it is most likely that you are keeping it well groomed and using quality external parasite repellents.

  The only time your Goldendoodle might have an infestation of lice or mites is when you first bring it home as a puppy, and you bought it from a pet store or an online advert. Lice and mites spread rapidly in unhygienic conditions.

  You will immediately see that your new Goldendoodle puppy's coat is dry or matted and that the skin is inflamed and flaky. Take your new puppy to your vet as soon as possible to get the right treatment to get rid of the infestation.

  If you have kept the puppy in a dog bed or allowed it onto your carpets and furniture, ask your vet what you must use on these items because lice and mites are tiny, prolific breeders and their eggs are very robust. Lice and mites spread easily to other pets, and some can spread to humans as well.

4. Health

If you bought your Goldendoodle puppy from a reputable breeder, you would have been given a copy of the genetic clearances of both the puppy's mother and father for predisposition to diseases that commonly occur in Golden Retrievers and Poodles.

If you bought your Goldendoodle puppy from a pet store or online advert you will not know if it has any genetic predisposition to certain health conditions. Genetic disease and health conditions your Goldendoodle may have inherited include:

- Allergies
- Addison's disease
- Elbow Dysplasia
- Eye disease
- Gastric Dilation-Volvulus
- Hip Dysplasia
- von Willebrand's Disease

These health conditions are covered in a bit more detail Chapter 1 which details the history and lineage of Goldendoodles.

5. Average Lifespan

Goldendoodles have an average lifespan of between 10 to 15 years.

The large sizes have a shorter lifespan than the small size.

For dog-lovers who have welcomed a Goldendoodle puppy into their home and made it part of their family, this lifespan seems too short. Time flies by and all too soon signs of ageing appear.

Greying appears around the face and muzzle, less activity, aching joints etc.

For many, a dog's life is too short, and ageing comes too soon.

Watching your Goldendoodle Age

You will have to face your Goldendoodle getting older.

For you, like thousands of people worldwide your Goldendoodle has not been merely a pet: it has been an important member of your family. Your Goldendoodle has become part of your daily routines, shares your homes and shares almost every aspect of your life.

Maybe you lovingly share individual quirks your Goldendoodle has, celebrate its birthday, or 'shame' it for being 'naughty' on various social media platforms. Your posts are always well received, commented on and shared.

Unfortunately, your Goldendoodle does not share the extended lifespan that humans have. Like all large dogs, large Goldendoodles have an average lifespan of 10 years, while smaller sizes seldom live beyond 15 years of age.

The average lifespan of any breed of dog is merely a guideline, and most dogs are considered as being "senior" by the age of 10. It is also around this age that you will start noticing changes in your Goldendoodle. Maybe it has become a bit slower, sleeps a bit longer, is starting to show signs of poor eyesight, its muscles are beginning to become less defined and are replaced by loser skin, and it's coat beginning to go grey. At first, it's hardly noticeable, but as time goes by ageing symptoms become more defined.

It is natural to want to ignore what you see, but in truth, you have to recognise signs of ageing in your Goldendoodle because the superficial signs may conceal more serious symptoms inside its body. Many internal signs of ageing like arthritis, tooth decay and internal organ disease can cause your Goldendoodle anything from mild discomfort to extreme pain.

In healthy older dogs, tooth decay can be fixed by having problem teeth extracted under anaesthetic, allowing your Goldendoodle to enjoy once again its meals and treats. Almost all vets are in favour of prescribing medication for pain control. There is no need for dogs to experience unnecessary pain, and many dogs continue to live happy lives on daily doses of medication for treatment of disease and pain control.

Because your Goldendoodle cannot tell you how it feels and does not experience the fear of disease that humans have, it is able to cope with internal pain and show few symptoms, so you may not necessarily notice anything untoward. Truth is, if your Goldendoodle could talk it would tell you that it's been having off days and not feeling too well over the last while.

When the vet diagnoses a fatal condition like cancer, kidney/liver/heart failure, tumours, etc. your shock of the diagnosis could be intense and the emotional pain so severe that you may go into a state of denial - refusing to accept. What are the treatment options? Only pain control and medicines to ease the symptoms? The condition is untreatable and ultimately fatal?

This experience will be genuinely traumatic, shocking and confusing. Letting go of a beloved member of your family is heartbreaking, and sometimes almost too painful to accept. It can leave you in a state of trauma, shock and confusion.

At some point you will have to make an excruciating decision; take your Goldendoodle home with strong medication and wait for it fade away, or opt for humane euthanasia. Either way, you will feel trapped! To keep your Goldendoodle alive because you cannot face the thought of it not being part of your life anymore could feel selfish. Humane euthanasia, on the other hand, could feel like you're betraying beloved member of your family.

Ultimately the decision will be yours, but you must remember that no vet would recommend humane euthanasia unless your Goldendoodle is going to experience substantial pain and discomfort before it eventually dies.

Also, bear in mind when making that decision, severe illness and suffering changes people physically, mentally and emotionally - and it will also change your Goldendoodle. The happy, loving, playful dog it was before will become lethargic, lose interest, possibly develop depression and have very little appetite. Your life together will never be the same again!

Whatever the choice you opt for, you will have to face the death of your beloved Goldendoodle; immediate or delayed, death is inevitable.

After the passing, you could experience a period of genuine grief and often guilt, no matter which option you chose.

Feelings and emotions are a natural part of the grieving process. Allow yourself time to grieve! In time you will accept your decision and feelings of sadness will be replaced with acceptance that you did what you believed was right at the time.

Love never dies and neither will the beautiful memories you will have of your Goldendoodle.

Dogs just leave this world far too soon!

Conclusion

There are many publications promoting Goldendoodles as the hot new breed on the block.

Unfortunately, these publications contain very few cautions and only highlight the positive traits new Goldendoodle owners can expect.

What they mainly focus on is the gorgeous looks of Goldendoodles, and yes they do look gorgeous.

But no dog should ever be brought home just because it looks cute or is beautiful. The fascination with its looks will wear off very quickly once you are battling to handle the dog.

Dogs must be brought home because you want a dog and the dog that you have chosen suits your lifestyle.

The majority of publications misrepresent Goldendoodles in three areas.

Firstly they refer to the Goldendoodles as having low shedding and even non-shedding coats. This is not true, and it misrepresents the breed. Goldendoodles are not an established breed, and low shedding is not guaranteed. As we have read, some Goldendoodles are low shedding, but many shed in line with their Golden Retriever genes.

This is a very dangerous misrepresentation because if a new Goldendoodle owner has specifically chosen the breed because it is low or non-shedding, they could end up with a dog that they don't want.

Secondly, most publications refer to Goldendoodles as friendly and easy to train, which they definitely are. But what they fail to mention is that Goldendoodles are highly intelligent and need to be part of a human family. They need constant interaction, play and stimulation with humans.

This can come as quite a shock to people who don't understand the implications of a dog that needs to be part of a human family. If the family is unwilling to incorporate the Goldendoodle into their daily life, they will end up with a 'problem-dog' on their hands.

Finally, they forget to mention that Goldendoodles can potentially grow into large thick-set strong dogs. This is a very important factor and another dangerous misrepresentation. Not all households are suited to big dogs.

All three of these misrepresentations can have disastrous consequences for Goldendoodles who end up unwanted and abandoned.

This book intends to make you aware of all the potential traits you can find in a Goldendoodle, positive and negative.

Now that you have finished reading this book you can make an educated decision rather than focus only on the good looks and all the hype around Goldendoodles.

Whether you choose to add a gorgeous Goldendoodle to your household or opt for a different breed of dog, may it become a valued family member and close companion.

Printed in Great Britain
by Amazon